Western Lights

a collection of short essays on buddhism

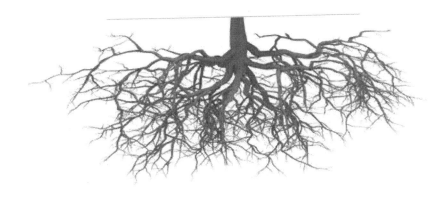

Western Lights

a collection of short essays on buddhism

Andrew Furst

STORY MERCHANT BOOKS
BEVERLY HILLS
2014

WESTERN LIGHTS
A Collection of Short Essays on Buddhism

ISBN 978-0-61567581-7

Author Website
www.andrewfurst.net

Story Merchant Books
9601 Wilshire Boulevard #1202
Beverly Hills CA 90210

http://www.storymerchant.com/books.html

Cover and interior design: Garrett Brown, Opaque Design & Print Production, Sudbury Vermont

Editor: Lisa Cerasoli

CONTENTS

ACKNOWLEDGMENTS

I'd like to thank my teachers Richard Sittinger, Peg Travers, Laurie Thibault, Geshe Tenley, Choden Rinpoche, and Dagri Rinpoche. I am also indebted to many others who have served as inspiration including His Holiness the Dalai Lama, Thich Nhat Hanh, Lama Surya Das, Sharon Salzburg, and Noah Levine. I'd also like to thank the Buddhist Meditation Group at the Unitarian Universalist Church of Reading for tolerating my instruction and ramblings.

I would like to gratefully recognize a group of good friends who took the time from their busy schedules to provide advice and editing for the first manuscript. Hearing their feedback was both encouraging and humbling. I'm much better off as an author having had their sage advice.

I thank John Intorcio and Sue Hall for really digging in with insightful and challenging questions. I appreciate Jennifer Brown's help in getting the manuscript in front of a publisher for some important perspective. As always, I enjoyed the feedback (especially in the realm of politics) of Dr. Jeff Everson. I was thrilled that some old friends from my raucous music days—Jason Dumont and Stephen Fulton—pitched in. Even high school friend, Carmen Beaulieu, joined the crowd. Finally, thank you to my contemporary friends Ann Fisher, Mary Lasdin, Sally Carroll, Katie Wheeler, Dawn Melissa Gonthier, Suzanne Mrozak, Fern

Barkalow, and Dr. Vonda Swartz.

Most of all I'd like to thank my family, the most important and best teachers of my life. Samantha, Ian, and Nathan: I love you.

INTRODUCTION

This collection of short essays was gleaned from my first foray into writing—blogging for the Buddhist Meditation Group at the Unitarian Universalist Church of Reading.

To those looking for insight on the path to writing a book, this was my route. In many ways, this book is a selfish venture. It has allowed me to see how everything and everyone are the Buddha teaching me. Writing has also allowed me to see my mind, mostly its cluttered nature, and to both adore it and strive to discipline it.

The blog has steered most recently onto the themes of naturalness, rhythms, and insights available in everyday life. I've strived to dust off the dry academic and culturally oriental tenets of this precious 2,500-year old religion and bring it to life. I've tried to do this by putting it through the agitator of the frenetic beat of western life and the wringer of the western reductionist mind.

The attempt is to take the familiar and spin it on its head in the hopes that I lure you, shake up your world view, and leave you with a little to chew on.

Amitabha Buddha

The Sanskrit word Amitabha is from the roots amita ("without bound, infinite") and ábhá ("light, splendor"). Another name for Amitabha is Amitáyus. Amitáyus is the compound of amita ("infinite") and áyus ("life").

The Chinese rendering of Amitabha's name is Amitofo. Amito are the first three syllables of Amitabha and Amitáyus. Fo is Chinese for Buddha. The Chinese rendering (Amitofo) wonderfully embraces both—meaning the Buddha of endless light and endless life.

Namo Amitofo
(I take refuge in Buddha Amitabha)

I What is the Single Most Important Teaching?

I had the opportunity to speak with students at Middlesex Community College in Bedford Massachusetts. I was invited by the professor to speak to a class on world art and literature about Buddhism. There were several delightfully engaged students.

One of them posed the following question:

> *Could you expand upon how Pure Land Buddhism differs from other schools? And what is its single most important teaching?*

Answer: Pure Land Buddhism rests on three pillars:

- Faith

- Vows

- Practice

Practice

During my visit to your class, we chanted, *"Namo Amitofo."* This is the practice—recalling the name of the Buddha.

The smaller Pure Land Sutra (a Sutra is analogous to a book in the Bible) states that if one chants the name of the Buddha with the sincere desire to be reborn in the Pure Land, that desire will be fulfilled.

That's a pretty unusual concept from a western perspective. Let me put it in terms that you can relate to: the most basic way to think about Buddha is not as a person or a god but as simply being awake to reality, to the world as it is.

The Pure Land practice is recalling our personal connection with the Buddha. There is a simple, yet profound peacefulness that is inherent in our nature. This peace is constantly accessible to us, even in the most troubling of times.

When we sit in meditation, we are closer than usual to the world as it is. By simply bringing body, breath, and mind together in the present moment, we touch Buddha; we touch reality, and we are in the world as it is. Most people's experience in this state is peaceful and rejuvenating.

Vows

By vows, I mean the commitment to the Eightfold Path. This is a commitment to wisdom, ethical living, and meditation. These three pillars can be broken down into the eight steps; right view, right intention, right speech, right action, right livelihood, right effort, right mindfulness, and right concentration.

Wisdom arises from the application of a disciplined mind to experience. We must live, eyes wide open, to reality. We must remember that if we look for happiness in a wish that things will turn out our way, we're going to be disappointed. We must commit to remove ourselves from the cycle of suffering that Buddhists call Samsara. To do so, we must discipline our minds to see things as they are, rather than how we want them to be.

Ethical Living is choosing honesty over deception, earning a living in a trade that offers a benefit to others, and acting with integrity. These activities are inherently a source of peace of mind. Further, honesty and integrity fosters relationships that are less likely to be sources of dissatisfaction.

Meditation is the regular practice of the examined life. It returns us to our natural state of balance. It provides the benefits of peace and centeredness, which in turn, motivate us to stay the course. Meditation supports our overall faith in the path of the Buddha.

Faith

Perhaps the most difficult Pure Land teaching is faith, but not because it's difficult to understand, because it is in contrast to how many of us think of "faith."

In the common understanding of the term, faith is a leap we take from the known to the unknown. Faith in God from a Judeo-Christian-Islamic sense is the bridge from our everyday experience to an intangible mystery.

This faith is often characterized as a weak point in religious philosophy, especially by those who see things from a scientific frame of reference. Atheists, like Richard Dawkins, who look at the world through the prism of science (a religion all its own), apply this criticism very effectively.

Faith from a Pure Land perspective is different. Faith arises directly from experience. The first two of the Buddha's foundational teachings called the Noble Truths, capture his great insight. First, we suffer from dissatisfaction, and second, it's something we do to ourselves.

Our faith is in this insight. It rests in the Buddha's admonishment that in order to be happy, we must escape the wheel of Samsara.

Samsara is like trying to flip a penny with the hopes that George Washington's face will land face up. It doesn't work the first time or the millionth time, but for some reason we keep trying.

Getting off the Wheel

Here's one way to think about Samsara. Say you want to go out for Thai. Your partner wants Mexican. What's your first emotion? Disappointment?

Where is this disappointment rooted? It is rooted in your desire to have things as you like them. When things don't turn out your way, you suffer disappointment.

The Buddha asks us to examine the situation. Is the disappointment worth it? How much better or worse would you be if you had Thai food when you wanted it? How long would you be happy if you got your way? In thirty minutes you might completely forget you had Thai, and instantly you'd be off, disappointed with the next thing. This is the hamster wheel of Samsara.

The Buddha says get off! Don't hitch your desire for happiness to things that don't offer real happiness in the first place.

This is Pure Land faith, faith in the causes and remedies for dissatisfaction. This is not faith in the unknown. It is faith in a very rational proposition based on experience.

Faith alone?

The practice of meditation allows us to take this faith even deeper. When we chant "Namo Amitofo," many, if not all of us, report a deep sense of peace. What happens?

We are in the present moment.

What does that mean?

In meditation, our focus is inward. We engage our faculties to observe our bodies, breath, and mind. At the first level, we temporarily disengage our relationship with others. It's valuable to recognize that our sense of individuality is in context to others. We are someone's child, someone's friend, someone's adversary. In meditation, we explore how our identity is deeply dependent on our relationship to the world.

At the next level, we change our relationship with our mind. We are usually driven by our thoughts. In meditation, we become the observer of thoughts. It's valuable to recognize that our sense of individuality is also connected to our thoughts. We are the person who believes this, or the person who has this opinion. In meditation, we explore how thoughts are not really who we are. In the same way, we explore our relationship to our bodies and our breath; we see how we are not really these things either.

In meditation, we experience peace and tranquility by developing a mature understanding of the adornments that we use to construct the self. We discover that contentment does not arise on the basis of "self." We learn that contentment arises from something else, something other than the self. In Buddhism, this is called Other Power, Amitofo, or the Buddha.

Meditation shows us that if we rely upon self for contentment, we will fail. But if we rest in "Other Power" it is always there for us. As we continue to meditate, we learn that peace is always available. We can return to it whenever we choose, and the only barrier is an unhealthy attachment to "self."

When we learn to have faith in Other Power, we gain the capacity to enjoy the contentment that arises from it. We discover that it is a bottomless well, an inexhaustible fountain of well-being.

Shinran, the founder of Shin Buddhism (a school of Pure Land), claimed that faith alone was all that was needed. Perhaps this is the most valuable teaching of Pure Land Buddhism.

Having faith in the path gives us the strength to continue. As we continue, we reap the benefits of the path. As we become more peaceful and well adjusted, we become better partners in relationships. As we improve our relationships, the benefits are passed on to others. As others benefit from our efforts, there is less suffering in the world.

When we sit in meditation, bringing body, breath, and mind into the present moment, we recognize that, in fact, we have always been in the Pure Land. This allows us to strengthen our faith—perhaps the most important teaching—in the aspiration to be awake.

2 How Do You Measure Enlightenment?

One of the more inquisitive members of our Sangha, our group of Buddhist practitioners, is a physicist. His approach to meditation is data driven and grounded in the scientific method. He reports regularly that he's experienced a few measurable benefits of the practice including a reduction in blood pressure.

While, in many respects, I share his empirical leanings, I believe there are things that can't be measured. Recently Lama Surya Das visited our Sangha to give a talk on Pure Land Buddhism. Afterwards, he offered time for questions and answers. My friend asked some great questions that cued Lama Surya Das to respond with references to current studies in neuroscience focused on the benefits of meditation.

At the end of the evening, my friend asked me, "How do you measure enlightenment?" Great question.

It's complicated. (Or is it?)

Satori, enlightenment, liberation, freedom from birth and death are some of the many terms used in the Buddhist lexicon to describe the goal of practice.

The Buddhist path is fundamentally about reflecting on our unhappiness. If we can identify the barriers to happiness, and remove them then we've succeeded. The epiphany is that happiness is simple (though not easy) to achieve.

Enlightenment, the great mysterious state of mind, is contentment, or freedom from suffering. How then do we measure happiness? We measure it in smiles, in the openness of our hearts, in generosity, in gratitude and compassion towards others, and in the steadiness of our contentment.

Keeping It Simple

In many ways, the myriad teachings of Buddhism are subtle and dense, and we can get lost in them. For this reason the masters are always quick to remind us, these are the teachings, not the goal. They are the finger pointing to the moon, not the moon itself.

When you sit on the cushion, when you do Qigong or yoga, when you chant, or when you're mindfully going about your day, the benefit is the feeling of satisfaction. *Contentment is the natural state that arises when we are deeply in touch with the miracle of now.* If you are happy as a result of Buddhist practice, then the teachings are working for you, and enlightenment is the result. If you are not, then the teachings are failing you, and you should stop.

Enlightenment is measured in contentment. Don't make it more complicated than that.

3 Buddhism: Spirituality for Atheists?

Our Sangha was visited by a very friendly woman who seemed excited to be there. She looked as though she had a flurry of questions, but she just didn't seem to know where to start.

To get things going, I asked the group the question, "What is your religious background?" The answer to this question is always informative and interesting to me. A person's relationship to their root religious tradition can tell me a lot about how to best approach introducing the Dharma. The new woman volunteered that she was an atheist.

This is not an uncommon response. After all, my Sangha is held at a Unitarian Universalist church. Unitarian Universalist congregations are often made up of people from diverse religious backgrounds including atheists, agnostics, and humanists. Buddhism seems to attract agnostics and atheists because it is often characterized as a philosophy rather than religion.

My personal religious background is Christianity, but as early as my teens, I leaned strongly towards atheism. I was puzzled by the portrayal of a God—who was apparently present in our lives but mysteriously absent from our experience. It was also not very difficult to reject a religious tradition that delivered the inquisition and Tammy Faye Baker.

Even today, I continue to believe that atheist thinkers like Jonathon Miller (producer of the *Atheism Tapes*), Colin McGinn, and even Richard Dawkins offer compelling questions and challenges to religious thinking that need to be considered.

Too often skepticism is met with circular arguments or the threat of eternal damnation, but questions and doubts are a natural part of the spiritual journey. There are different types of doubt. Some are critically important.

The "Question"

So how does one introduce the Dharma to an atheist? The Buddha himself offered little explanation when it came to the question, *does God exist?* When confronted with the question directly, he was said to have maintained a strict silence.

I find this approach attractive. It was especially appealing when I was tilting away from Christianity. The Buddha set aside the questions that seemed to lead to absurdity and focused on more immediate issues like happiness:

- Who am I?
- How do I live a good life?

I think this makes Buddhism palatable for atheists. Perhaps it is the desire to move on from the God question. At the bare minimum, we're silent on the issue.

Inside Out

Separating the God question from Buddhism does not make Buddhists atheists—within silence lies mystery. That doesn't mean, however, we should infer from this acknowledgement of the mystery a nod one way or another on the matter of the divine.

The Buddhist tradition is introspective. The exploration of self is fruitful in both practical and religious ways. As we deconstruct the self, we gain insight into our personal barriers to happiness, and our relationships to those around us.

As we internalize the teachings of *anatta* or not-self, we encounter the mystery. In interdependence, we discover gratitude. In the present moment, we discover the sacred.

In the teaching of not-self, we must contend with the paradox of an undiscoverable "I" Emptiness confronts us with life shattering doubts about who we are. Buddhism, with its message of oneness, speaks of a single, boundless, interconnected being in which we all dwell. This hearkens to the Apostle Paul's message: *"For in him we live and move and have our being."* (Acts 17:28)

For this reason, I often make it a point to offer parallels to Christian mystical theology when talking about the Dharma and the experiences we have in meditation. If someone rejects this wisdom wholesale because it hints at something religious, then they suffer from the same dogmatism that plagues the blindly religious.

The exploration the Buddha prescribes must be without bias. I urge people to explore the effect that rejecting religion might have in their search for answers.

Agreeing How to Disagree

I share with atheists a deep skepticism of literal readings of scripture. The Buddhist Sutras are filled with references to gods, demi-gods, and demons. They are subject to the same literal reading.

When atheists and theists clash, they tend to do so on the framework of a fairly literal interpretation of scripture. Atheists effectively discredit fundamentalism but improperly claim victory over all religion. When theists adopt the framework of the atheist's critique by defending literalism, they do a disservice to all.

Arguing the existence of God is a fruitless effort. If we are looking to demonstrate something out of reach of shared experience, the argument will remain forever unresolved. If we are looking to employ logic to infer a deity, we fall into absurdity.

Did our ancestors need to tell us the creation story? Yes, it is a way to answer the questions: *Who am I? How do I fit in?* Do scriptures offer an accurate timeline and sequence of events or do they tell us a story that offers insight into the human condition?

Silent Reverence

There is a powerful wisdom in the silence of the Buddha on the matter of God. It's attractive to skeptics and those struggling with their relationship to the divine. As I said earlier, the silence sets aside the problems with fundamentalist theology, while leaving open the big questions.

The path of the Buddha offers a hint of the mystery based on experience. We are led to see that life is being in concert with nature's unfolding. Spiritual practice, as St. Francis of Assisi put it, is the process of "looking for what is looking."

> "God is an intelligible sphere, whose center is everywhere, and whose circumference is nowhere."
>
> Alain of Lille, 12th Century Theologian

While I am careful to acknowledge the silence of the Buddha on the mystery, the words attributed to Alain of Lille never fail to bring a smile to my face.

4 Ten Steps to Paradise

I've arrived at that age when death begins to speak more regularly to me. I work for an oncology diagnostic company. I hear patient stories every day, happy and sad. People around me speak of friends and family passing much more frequently than I remember.

As a youth, I felt that religion was for old people who were afraid of dying. I don't think I was wrong. Death is a wake-up call, though it shouldn't be just for old people.

What does happen at death?

Can we affect what happens to us when we die?

The essence of the Pure Land teachings comes to a very simple point. If you recite the name of the Buddha, even 10 times, with the sincere aspiration to be reborn in the Pure Land, at death Amitabha Buddha will usher you to Sukhavati, or what you might call Buddhist heaven.

Well, that's easy! Except what does it mean? When I first grappled with Pure Land, I got caught at the word "reborn." We're talking about reincarnation aren't we? What's that all about?

Heaven, really?

To be honest, I was not immediately receptive to Pure Land Buddhism or the idea of Sukhavati. Coming to Buddhism with an aversion to many Christian doctrines, then joining a Sangha that aspired to go to Buddhist heaven didn't seem like a good fit.

My initial strategy was to practice my own form of Buddhism, which would be tailored specifically and more intellectually suited for my needs. I'd join the Sangha and keep silent my opinions about this simple-minded approach to enlightenment! Even better, great Buddhist teachers like Thich Nhat Hahn offered sophisticated versions of Pure Land practice that spoke to my "more advanced understanding." And with a little practice on my own, I'd awaken fully and be living in the Pure Land in no time. No teleportation to some distant galaxy or another lifetime was needed for this Bodhisattva.

But—and you probably knew this was coming—I was wrong. My change of heart came about in part from a gradual understanding of rebirth and the understanding that my ego is the biggest obstacle to peace.

The Pure Land is really here and now, when you are truly awake.

Rebirth

> "Everyone has a worldview. Whether or not we realize it, we all have certain presuppositions and biases that affect the way we view all of life and reality."
>
> ChristianWorldview.net

Reincarnation is a concept that seems to belong to the east. But it is analogous to western thought on the afterlife. It's another way to look at the mystery of death.

A central tenet of Christian doctrine is the afterlife. The fruits of faith come in the form of eternal life in heaven. The opportunity for salvation offers great hope and motivation to the faithful. It forms the basis of a worldview that is fulfilling and encourages us to play well together.

Similarly, the worldview of reincarnation is extremely motivating and liberating. If we can settle into the idea that our current lifetime is just one of many, then the maddening rush to accomplish everything melts away. From another perspective, by recognizing that this is our home for all time, we become motivated to make it a better place.

Who is Reborn?

I don't know about you, but I don't remember any past lives. What exactly is meant by reincarnation?

In Tibetan Buddhism, there is a tradition of seeking out the next incarnation of beloved teachers. Through astrology and other divination techniques, the reincarnated being is identified. The discovered child is then restored to the position they held in their previous life.

But what passes on from lifetime to lifetime? Is it a particular personality or physical trait? For example, the Dalai Lama looks nothing like his predecessor. He has different preferences and habits. He probably has a slightly different take on Buddhism than his previous incarnation. If these traits aren't what continue on, what does?

What survives death? The Western answer is the soul. We usually think of the soul in the context of our ego. In the model offered in Dante's *Divine Comedy*, our person, in some eternal form, is consigned to heaven, hell, or purgatory.

But can our eternal soul exist on the level of the ego? Is the soul a physical, mental, or emotional thing? Bodies change, mental states are ever shifting, and emotions fly all over the place. Are these things the stuff of eternity?

Some kind of transformation is required. The impermanent aspects of self must somehow be transformed to something permanent.

This leads to a conundrum. If our soul is eternal, in what form would it take? Would we live forever in the state we were in just prior to death, or as a child, or maybe at a particularly happy time in our life?

Of course we don't have answers to any of these questions. But we are driven to consider the possibilities. We have to be careful in our approach to the afterlife, because in both the east and the west, it's critical to our worldview. We should consider what we can know, before taking a leap.

Where Do We Go From Here?

For Buddhists, answers are found within. We are challenged to examine ourselves closely to gain insight on life's big questions. This is the exercise of meditation.

There are traditionally two forms of Buddhist meditation, Vipassana (insight) and Samatha (tranquility). We can engage the former, and ask ourselves the question, *What about us could possibly survive death?* Meditating on this, we can learn a great deal. We discover, over and over, that nearly everything about us is transient: our thoughts, our habits, our bodies.

But, there is one thing that is different. Witness to thoughts, emotions, and sensations is the underlying state of being. Tibetans call this Rigpa: pure awareness.

Perhaps this is the *me* that our religious ancestors are talking about. Perhaps this is the *me* that survives death. Pure awareness and the egocentric concept of soul differ in that Rigpa is without form. My Rigpa and yours are indistinguishable. Being doesn't bear any of the characteristics we'd use to distinguish one person from the next. If Rigpa is the soul, then it removes the ego from the afterlife equation.

Endless Life, Endless Light

If we accept that awareness pervades all sentient beings and is indistinguishable across individuals, can we accept that it also pervades all beings across time?

Of course questions remain unanswered. While my awareness is indistinguishable from yours, does that mean they are the same? Is awareness eternal, or does it extinguish at death? These are barriers to an acceptance of reincarnation on a rational basis.

Bringing our mind to the name of the Buddha Amitabha, we are reminded of the wellspring of light and life that is shared by all sentient beings. Remembering that all life is finite (impermanent) and deeply dependent (not-self) on others reminds us that we are not separate, but deeply connected on every level. Amongst all beings, we intimately share everything. Awareness is one of those things.

Death is a fact of life. If the Buddha teaches us anything, it is that clinging to an egocentric notion of self is the cause and perpetuator of suffering. Relying on the power of self will fail us in our efforts towards liberation. Perhaps in death we leave a lifetime of these notions behind. Born again we might carry on in the world we shaped in the last life. If we've left behind a better world, all beings will benefit. Sounds like paradise.

5 Going Toward the Light

I'd like to spend some time talking about Pure Land Buddhism directly, since it's the core of my own practice and that of our Sangha.

Pure Land is the most popular form of Buddhism in China and in all of Asia. Pure Land, or Ching T'u, is focused on the aspiration to be reborn in the Western Pure Land of Buddha Amitabha.

The Ching T'u School traces its teachings to Sakyamuni Buddha as found in the three Pure Land or Sukhavati Sutras.

- Longer Pure Land Sutra

- Shorter Pure Land (or Amitabha) Sutr

- Amit yus Meidation Sutra

The tradition tells us that once we're reborn in Amitabha's Sukhavati (Land of Bliss), we cannot regress on the path to liberation and we will achieve it in one lifetime. We are reborn on a lotus flower, surrounded by Bodhisattvas, and immersed in the Dharma. The trees, birds, and wind sing to us; all is impermanent, all compound things have no self, and Nirvana awaits us.

Western Heaven

The main method of cultivation in Pure Land is chanting the name of the

Buddha, *Namo Amitofo*. The practice finds its source in the Longer Pure Land Sutra. The Sutra tells the story of the Bodhisattva Dharmakara, who, upon fulfilling 48 vows, attains perfect enlightenment and becomes Buddha Amitabha. His fulfillment of vows 18 and 19 offer us the means to be reborn in the Pure Land.

> 18. O Bhagavat, if, when I attain Buddhahood, sentient beings in the lands of the ten quarters who sincerely and joyfully entrust themselves to me, desire to be born in my land, and call my Name, even ten times, should not be born there, may I not attain perfect Enlightenment.

> 19. O Bhagavat, if, when I attain Buddhahood, sentient beings in the lands of the ten quarters, who awaken aspiration for Enlightenment, do meritorious deeds and sincerely desire to be born in my land, should not, at their death, see me appear before them surrounded by multitude of sages, may I not attain perfect Enlightenment.

Faith in Amitabha, calling his name, awakening the aspiration for Enlightenment, and the sincere desire for rebirth in the Pure Land are the ways to reach this western heaven. From here, your path to liberation is secured. The similarity to faith and works in western traditions is not hard to see.

Damn Good Advice

Be good, have faith, and aspire to go to heaven. Really, what better advice is there?

The Buddha offered the eightfold path as a guide to good living. He made it clear that liberation was possible, and he offered us a rationale "why" we should have faith in the path. These are known as the fourth, second, and third Noble Truths, respectively.

A commitment to this aspiration is one reason we recite the Buddha's name each day.

Other Power vs. Self Power

One of the pillars of the Buddha's message is that all things—objects, relationships and people—are subject to constant change. The complimentary observation the Buddha made was if we want lasting contentment, we cannot put our faith in things that do not last, especially ourselves.

Temporary things do not provide contentment. This statement is backed up by a lifetime of evidence. For example let's consider a car. In a matter of years, a new car becomes an old car. It costs money to maintain, breaks down and eventually it's discarded. The happiness associated with buying a new car is short lived and ultimately replaced with indifference, or worse, regret.

Are our bodies and egos any different from a car? We are acutely aware that we are aging and dying. We are constantly challenged with self-doubt because of our failures and mistakes. Yet the delusion that the temporary pleasures can provide contentment persists. Despite all the evidence, we resist the effort to look deeper and change our approach to contentment.

But Socrates reminded us that the unexamined life is not worth living. If we choose to look deeper, slowly and surely we begin to see how this delusion prevents us from living in a way that can be authentic and satisfying. We do this by asking questions and being open to their answers.

The Name That Calls

The Sanskrit word Amitabha is from the roots amita ("without bound, infinite") and ábhá ("light, splendor"). Another name for Amitabha is Amitáyus. Amitáyus is the compound of amita ("infinite") and áyus ("life").

The Chinese rendering of Amitabha's name is Amitofo. Amito are the first three syllables of Amitabha and Amitáyus. Fo is Chinese for Buddha. The Chinese rendering (Amitofo) wonderfully embraces both—meaning the Buddha of endless light and endless life.

Chanting the name of the Buddha offers many benefits. As a mantra, it allows us to bring our minds and bodies to a single point of focus. As we sit, we can always draw our attention back to the recitation of the Buddha's name. Our senses can also be immersed in the sound, vibration, activity, and thought of Amitofo. This can bring on a deep state of tranquility.

I invite you to do this for even five minutes. At the end of the chapter I'll provide a simple meditation to get you started. These five minutes can bring an immediate sense of well-being and peace. If you enjoy it, continue to do it every day. Soon, you will begin to look forward to it. Slowly, over time, this sense of peace will spill over into your life.

Where does this benefit arise from? The answer is Buddha Amitabha.

Who is the Doctor and What is the Medicine?

On the surface, it is easy to see why meditation is beneficial. It's quality down time. Meditation is an opportunity to check out from the constant barrage of things to do, crises to solve, and regrets to ponder. When you simply settle into the present and concentrate on being, these things begin to melt away.

Chanting the name of the Buddha allows your body and mind to return to the present. In this sense *Namo Amitofo* is a mind guard—one meaning of the Sanskrit word mantra. It is a protector, guarding us from the mental distraction that prevents us from being in the present moment. By providing us a means to be present, it allows us to rejuvenate and heal.

On another level, it provides insight into our true nature. As we begin to notice the transient nature of our thoughts, we begin to see what the Buddha meant by compound things. For instance, thoughts can arise in our mind as a result of outside stimulus. They can occur in response to other thoughts, or they just simply arise in the moment.

As we become more and more familiar with ourselves through meditation, we realize the transience of every aspect of our bodies, thoughts, and personalities. We develop a deep appreciation and respect for them. But we also begin to understand that they are fading and will ultimately fail us.

Meditating on the realization that our bodies and minds are transient can introduce conundrums like:

Who am I?

Who is calling out the name of the Buddha?

Who is chanting Namo Amitofo?

Not Self

Amitofo is the Buddha of endless light and endless life. As the Buddha of life, he represents the heart of reality that infuses the universe with life. From generation to generation, from amoeba to human, Amitofo is the persistent and eternally present life of the universe.

As the Buddha of light, Amitabha represents the light and life that are the beacons at the center of every living being.

Who is calling Namo Amitofo?

Latitude and Longitude?

Where is the Pure Land of Amitabha? In our hectic and stressed lives, it is far, far away. It's in another lifetime, where we might have the time to meditate more often and live the examined life.

But when we are immersed in life, in the here and now, how are we separate and different from Amitabha? Isn't he attending to our very lives and showing us our liberation? Isn't he illuminating this very body, in this very moment?

Perhaps the Pure Land is not so far away. Maybe it's right behind us, in our blind spot as we drive relentlessly forward in life pursuing the next goal or achievement.

Perhaps we should spend a few minutes each day chanting the name of the Buddha. Try it now.

A Short Meditation

Meditation is the unification of body, breath, and mind. During this brief session I encourage you to leave everything else behind.

Let's start with the body. Find a comfortable sitting posture or even lie down. You want to be able to relax all the big muscles in your body. Close your eyes or keep them open as you feel most comfortable.

Spend a minute to reacquaint yourself with all your parts. Take a deep inhale in and with a slightly exaggerated exhale, release all the muscles of your body. Sink. Let all of your flesh literally hang off of your bones. For the next five breaths allow this sense of relaxation to deepen, letting go a little more with each exhale.

Now we'll synchronize the breath and the mind. You can choose to chant silently or out loud (I recommend out loud — think Gregorian Chant). Either way start with a deep inhale. On the exhale, chant Namo Amitofo slowly for the length of the breath.

Inhale again, and exhale Namo Amitofo. If your chanting aloud, use a deep low tone. Feel the vibration from your throat and heart. Allow it to expand up and down your spinal column. If you're chanting silently, allow the words to permeate through your entire body.

Continue to inhale and chant Namo Amitofo for seven, twenty-one, or twenty-eight breaths. Or count on your fingers in intervals of ten.

After your final chant, come to complete silence. Allow your body and mind to settle and take stock of how you feel.

Pause as long as you'd like, drink in the feeling.

6 Dancing With the Ever Changing Universe

During our weekly Sangha meetings we practice gentle qigong movements to help unite our body, breath, and mind. As we do the movements, I recite a poem written by my teacher, Richard Sittinger:

My spirit is made of light,

From Tao it arises, the bright, morning sun.

In all directions it shines, there are no impediments.

My body arises from earth, five elements, in perfect embrace.

From the union of sunlight yang, and moonlight yin,

My mind arises, day and night, there is peace.

Taking all sentient beings, into my heart,

In loving embrace, dancing with the ever changing universe,

Is the breath of wisdom.

Union with all things is the supreme way.

I really enjoy this poem. I encourage the Sangha members to read it, because from my perspective everything is in there. It is a succinct summary of the Buddha's way. It's truly a gem.

The language is Taoist. Taoism is a sister religion to Buddhism in China, it is the source of Qigong, Feng Shui and other Chineses traditions. By using Taoist concepts and language, my teacher nicely reflects the amorphous nature of Buddhism.

As Buddhism moves from one place to the next, it has the capacity to assimilate and be assimilated by the cultures it lives in.

In China, Taoism, Confucianism, and Buddhism have a blurred and symbiotic relationship. Each has absorbed elements of the others. The Buddha taught that there are 84,000 Dharma doors. By this he meant we can each come to enlightenment in our own unique way. Our awakening arises out of our own particular forms of suffering and realization. The 84,000 Dharma doors open as they are needed and China is a good example of how this has happened.

The Three Bodies

The poem by my teacher brings beautiful focus to the three aspects of our being: body, breath, and mind. However you choose to call them or view them, they are always there for us to enjoy.

In our Qigong practice, we unite our body, breath, and mind. This brings peace of mind. It allows us to release the stress of the week, by returning to the place where our senses live right here, right now. The rest, for now, can fall away.

Walking the Walk

But as we go about life after sitting, we are quickly drawn back to unmindfulness and stress. How can we walk this walk outside the quiet setting of a Sangha meeting? We can do it by being in our three bodies at work, at play, and in hard times.

My spirit is made of light,

From Tao it arises,

The bright, morning sun.

Amitabha Buddha is the Buddha of endless light and endless life. The endless light of Buddha Amitabha is our first body. It is our spirit and the spirit of all sentient beings. It is our true self.

To put a simple name to it, it is being, it is life. After all we are human beings.

Seeing ourselves as endless light or as pure awareness can be a little counter intuitive. But the Buddha tells us seeing ourselves any other way is the cause of dissatisfaction.

This is the second noble truth: attachment to the self and other temporary things is the cause of suffering. Everything about our so-called self—our bodies, beliefs, and opinions—can and do change. Watch the power of "If" in action. This is attachment to self:

- If we identify with our body, we see that the body will die and we begin to fear death.

- If we identify with our opinions, when others dispute them, we feel angry.

- If we identify with our beliefs, and they change, we doubt ourselves and suffer.

When we liberate ourselves from these distortions, we become free to shine, to open our hearts.

In all directions it shines,

There are no impediments.

What, then, is true about us in a lasting permanent way? We are beacons of awareness.

It courses through our bodies as we quiet our mind and turn our focus inwards. This awareness is our connection to the world, and it's a channel for nourishment. We cannot separate ourselves from this light. It is our true self. This awareness is the endless light of Buddha Amitabha. It illuminates everything and everything unfolds in its light.

My body arises from earth,

Five elements, in perfect embrace.

The second aspect of being is our physical body and surroundings. The world around us unfolds before our senses. Our true self, *light,* is manifest in the forms of our bodies, relationships, and the activities of our daily lives.

In our Qigong practice, this unfolding is the movement of the forms. As we focus on our breath and the activities of our bodies we are dancing in harmony. This union, or yoga, is a source of peace and of great enjoyment.

The wonder of our bodies and our planet are endlessly breathtaking—because they do not last. They are precious for that reason. By doing our Qigong, we are becoming deeply in touch with the present moment, appreciating the preciousness of each form, discovering their true nature and learning to take care of our bodies and our world.

From the union of sunlight yang, and moonlight yin, my mind arises,

Day and night, there is peace.

As we become more in tune with our body, breath, and mind, we discover the natural rhythms of life. We develop an appreciation of the ebb and flow of emotions, friendships, and well-being. There is darkness and light in our lives, always changing. We recognize that we are dancing.

Simultaneously embracing this precious world and acknowledging its fleeting nature, we can see the yin and yang of this life as notes in a song—our heartbeat, our breath, the rhythms of the moment are instruments that play together, creating the song. It is unfolding before us forever. This is eternal and spirited life.

Taking all sentient beings, into my heart,

In loving embrace,

Seen through the lens of attachment, life and its dissatisfactions are relentless. But clearly seeing life (by removing the lens of attachment), we see it is the dance of heaven. From the wisdom earned from a lifetime of dissatisfaction, we naturally develop heartfelt compassion for others. What else could we possibly feel?

This natural well of compassion within us is the heart of the Buddha. Uncovering it and cultivating it is a great accomplishment and a treasure. It is the key to a satisfying life.

Dancing with the ever changing universe,

Is the breath of wisdom.

As we rediscover our true selves, we remove the obstructions to illumination, enlightenment. We see life's preciousness. We become attuned to its rhythms, and we begin to enjoy the unfolding dance of life.

Union with all things is the supreme way.

7 Pull Yourself Together

Pull yourself together. It's one of those awkward, figurative colloquialisms like, *pick yourself up by your boot straps.* The irony of these phrases is perhaps appropriate to the situations they apply to. It's an impossible task, yet we know exactly how to do it. You can often find great wisdom buried in these idioms.

What would you pull to be together? What do we need to succeed? Our bodies, our mind and the breath that binds them together are all and everything we need. Anything else is just fluff.

Doing our Qigong is a way of pulling ourselves together—bringing your mind to your body and your breath. Where those three aspects unite, Peace is always there. *"For goodness sake, pull yourself together!"*

8 Super Special Secret Sauce

Many Buddhist teachings are formulated to help us nurture the characteristics of enlightened beings. For example Lojong and loving kindness practices engage the student in the emulation of wisdom and compassion. It's not enough to know that compassion is good for you; you have to put it to use in daily life. The methods train the mind and body in much the same way we learn to play a musical instrument, through frequent repetition. After a certain number of iterations, the motions become natural.

They help you walk the walk. Here is one of the practices I enjoy.

The Sauce

Often times when I sit for meditation, as part of my preparation, I settle into my posture, take inventory of my body and emotion tone, and then I do a little special *yoga*.

Try it yourself. While you're reading this, sit down and comfortably settle yourself. Put your feet flat on the ground. Take a nice deep inhale and let it out. You may want to do this a few times, because it really feels great.

Find a comfortable balance in your spine, settling one vertebra atop the other. Then scan your body for tension. Come to a posture that allows you to release as much tension in your body as possible for the duration of this short exercise.

Now that you've settled your body, release the tension in your face. Let your cheekbones relax, the skin of your temples, and your forehead. Let your teeth separate slightly. Allow the pores of your scalp to open and your skin to become completely receptive to your surroundings.

Now, let this release propagate throughout your entire body. Slowly let awareness and openness radiate down your torso and arms. Stop briefly at a few checkpoints to nourish each part with the spaciousness. Let your throat bask in it. Then move slowly down to your heart, solar plexus, and the space between your shoulder blades. Feel the openness expand to your kidneys, stomach, lower abdomen and back. Let it settle at the point where your body makes contact with the chair or whatever you're sitting on. Finally, let it wash down your thighs, calves, shins, ankles and feet.

Give it a few seconds and enjoy the feeling of openness and ease.

Finally, bring a gentle smile to your lips. Notice how it feels. Your body and your emotions will recognize the cue. If it's working, continue on, perhaps to a full out smile. Don't overdo it. Just let it blossom. Maybe a funny memory is jarred loose. Go with it. Smile with your whole body. Feel your heart lighten and your spine lengthen.

If you've got it in you, dare to laugh. Maybe start with a giggle and see if it catches. Let yourself go.

Happiness Is as Happiness Does

This little meditation offers benefits on two levels. First you feel better during and after the experience. Second it offers you a little insight into happiness. It can arise in response to something funny, like when you hear a joke. But conversely, emulating the behavior of laughing, you can evoke happiness and well-being. Interesting observation.

There is a lot packed into that insight, enough to explore across a lifetime. Meditation is finding the seeds of a rich life within and germinating them. It's a noble practice that is beneficial to you and everyone around you. It's a wellspring available to all. Drink from it.

9 Meditation on Hope

In one respect, hope is an enemy. Hope is an attachment to an imagined future. We suffer disappointment when our hopes are dashed.

But hope for a satisfying life is our motivation. The reason we go on is the desire for lasting contentment. So hope is also our friend. A right understanding of hope is important.

Dancing

Sitting in meditation is a dance. We have a partner of sorts. As we embark on sitting, each moment brings something new. There are itches, distractions, surprises, and adjustments. All the sensations of these passing moments are our partners, our companions in this dance.

When we meditate we are dancing with each moment. Just like the very first dance we remember: We are self-conscious, but eager. We hope for a connection, but we're cautious of intimacy.

Our ideas about meditation are just like our ideas about people. We build stories that are filled with expectations, worries, and aspirations. There is always mystery involved in becoming intimate with another person. Their stories are a secret and, once revealed, don't often live up to our expectations. It's a risk.

Personal Stories

Our stories aren't just about other people. We have our own narratives. They can be satisfying or they can weigh us down. Our stories accumulate, change, and fade as we need them to. These stories are our resumes, convictions...and, in many ways, our obituaries.

But in an important way, we need to see our stories for what they are. Our biographies are never complete, and always suffer from a lack of perspective.

The Power of Our Stories

Success depends on our stories. If our narrative includes being a Harvard Business School graduate, we're likely to enjoy wealth and luxury. But if our story is that of failure, we tend to live out that story.

Stories shape our consciousness and our actions. They are the prism we look through and the bias we use to justify our actions.

When we sit in meditation, each moment presents a new story. Whether we enjoy it depends on us. It depends on how we are looking, how we receive it when it enters our consciousness.

The Quality of Experience

When we're meditating, we have the opportunity to observe our narratives as they play out. The power they hold over us directly affects the quality of our experience. When we are slaves to our stories, our experience is narrow and tight. When we develop perspective into our stories and learn that we can exercise power over them, our quality of experience changes. *This is a hint at the freedom that is available to us.*

Right Hope

Hope in the form of a preference for something is suffocating. It holds power over us. It leads to discontent in the form of unmet expectations. It's a story that risks a bad ending.

Hope as an aspiration for contentment, openness, and enlightenment can put us in the driver's seat. The desire to be available to the present moment and the pleasure it holds is a noble one.

What I hope for you is the aspiration to openness towards experience. I hope you can find the freedom that comes with knowing your stories belong to you, not the other way around.

Intimacy is standing before your partner, accepting and giving fully. Meditation is intimacy with each moment and everything that arises in it. The story unwinds itself—the pleasure is found in being there as it unfolds.

10 Stop Practicing Buddhism (And Just Do It)

I was paralyzed. It was like being thrown helpless into a fire. Some distant circumstance fueled her anger and my presence was just kindling for the inferno. I was in the wrong place at the right time.

In a fifth grader's life there are lots of rules and I'd done a pretty good job keeping up with them. But this one was about to be a problem: don't ever hit a girl.

She grabbed me in a headlock, dropped her body and pulled me to the ground. She didn't hurt me, but I was stunned. I tried to wrestle loose, push her away, and escape to some safe distance. But she was determined.

I don't remember her name or much else about that day, but the memory of utter powerlessness remains. Boys just can't hit girls. There is no caveat for when a girl strikes first. All I could do was give up. I fell limp and waited for the teacher to separate us.

To add insult to injury, I was left to face the ridicule of my peers. To any onlooker, it was a fight, and I lost. But it wasn't fair.

Rules

Almost as persistent as gravity, is the yearning to answer questions like, *How can I live a good and happy life?* On some level, we settle on a set of rules and assumptions, a religion or a philosophy, that put us right with how we make our living and carry on our relationships. But at best, those philosophies are slippery and unpredictable.

The influence these choices have over our lives is powerful. They are the moral framework in which we act. When our assumptions are challenged, or found lacking, we are often stunned. Some of the benchmarks of growing up are the struggles we have filling the gaps that rules don't address. My fifth grade brush with involuntary pacifism was that kind of experience.

My oldest son is learning how to drive. He just got his permit. When we're out driving, I can tell he prefers to have clear rules, especially after rough patches. He doesn't have the experience to draw on to make good judgments, or to make them "on the fly," like one does when driving.

What gives me confidence that he's going to be OK is when I see him take his personal experiences and shape them into good decisions. Experience is the best teacher. This is true for driving, and not hitting girls, and for putting our religion or philosophy into practice.

Experience

The Buddha prescribed a way to live a full and happy life: The Eightfold Path. It's both the rules of the game and the prize.

The Eightfold Path has three dimensions: the wisdom aspect, the ethical aspect and the mental development aspect.

Wisdom

Wisdom, Right View, and Intention. Learning starts by seeing life in the light of the noble truths. You have to work to extinguish the habit of looking for happiness in the wrong places.

Ethical Aspect

Right Speech, Action, and Livelihood. You (have to) make an effort to be kind in speech and actions. Find an ethical means to make a living.

Mental Development

Right Effort, Mindfulness, and Concentration. Through effort, mindfulness, and concentration we develop the discipline of mind to see clearly. Seeing clearly allows us to secure the virtues of wisdom and compassion, the two attributes of awakened beings.

As a beginner you rely on the eight points (wisdom, right view, right intention, right speech, right action, right livelihood, right effort, right mindfulness, and right concentration) to guide you. But when you look back on them after years of practice, you realize they describe the nature of enlightenment.

Ironically, having cultivated these virtues, we look back on the eightfold path and the contentment it affords us and wonder, *how could we have desired to act any differently?*

Doing It

With each turn and stop light, my son becomes more adept at driving. He develops the ability to skillfully respond to surprises. The rules helped form the foundation, but the experience is what becomes good driving.

When I look back on my fifth grade playground tussle, I see it through older eyes and I understand I wasn't equipped to handle the circumstances. While I had the rules right, I didn't have the experience to handle the situation skillfully.

Religion and philosophy can serve as a wonderful foundation with which to build a rich and well-lived life upon. But unless we engage the precepts in experience, we miss the point. Buddhism's primary exhortation is to walk the walk. For me, sitting in meditation and mindfulness in daily life are infinitely more useful than reading or talking about the rules of Buddhism.

Reading or talking about Buddhism helps to form and reinforce a foundation of understanding. But remember, nothing will move you more towards a fulfilling life than putting the path into practice. Only then, through the challenges and missteps that come with walking the walk, will your real life begin.

11 Buddhism: Religion, Belief System, or Philosophy

Question: *I've read that Buddhism is not so much a religion as it is a belief system. Since I don't know a lot about Buddhism, what are your thoughts on that?*

I wouldn't characterize Buddhism as a belief system.

The definition of belief is:

- An acceptance that a statement is true or that something exists.

- Something one accepts as true or real; a firmly held opinion or conviction.

In contrast to belief, there is knowledge. To know is defined as:

- To be aware of through observation, inquiry, or information.

- Have knowledge or information concerning.

The Buddha's teaching is grounded in experience. Belief, which by definition is conspicuously void of inquiry, is not. The Buddha insisted that verification is necessary, and instructed us to avoid belief.

Is Buddhism a Religion?

The etymology of the word religion links it to the French *religare* meaning "to bind fast," to "place an obligation on," or a "bond between humans and gods."

You can draw an analogy between the western notion of religion and the Vedic tradition of yoga. The term *yoga* means "to yoke" like to yoke oxen or yoking, as in a union, or yoking oneself to a discipline. On par with the notion "to bind fast," the yogic tradition seeks union with the divine. Religion and yoga share this aspiration.

While Buddhism is fairly silent on the topic of a deity, it behaves like a religion. There are rituals and institutions, worship and salvation. The fundamental Buddhist notion of impermanence imbues every moment with sanctity. In Buddhism, achieving union with the divine is touching each moment with mindfulness and gratitude.

The Buddha's path is a yogic path. If we allow the analogy between yoga and religion, then Buddhism is a religion.

Is Buddhism a Philosophy?

> "Believe nothing, no matter where you read it, or who said it, no matter if I have said it, unless it agrees with your own reason and your own common sense."
>
> The Buddha

A more prevalent idea is that Buddhism is a philosophy.

Philosophy is defined literally as loving knowledge, from philo, "loving" + sophia, "knowledge or wisdom." This jibes perfectly with the Buddha's instruction to believe nothing, but to seek the truth, to be in contact with what actually *is*.

Philosophy is about ideas. Ideas are theories about reality. We construct theories about reality so we might live in right relationship to it, to find balance. The goal of seeking harmony is happiness, or at least less suffering. Theories are born out, or fail, based on how they correspond to experience.

The Buddha's foundational sermon, the Four Noble Truths, prescribes a theory on how to live in harmony with the world. The goal is to reduce suffering.

So it is not a stretch to consider Buddhism a philosophy.

Union

I think it's useful to see Buddhism as both a religion and a philosophy. Our spiritual practice and theories must not contradict experience. As a philosophy, Buddhism is pragmatic and focused on knowledge and results. But if we unpack it a little, Buddhism leads us to see that the world is sacred.

Siddhartha Gautama found that we come to the sacred through unobstructed contact with reality. Beliefs and untested ideas that we hold in our heads, do not lead us there.

12 What's the Deal With Karma?

Question: Isn't there always a leap of faith that is required with all religions? Must one be willing to accept something that can't be proven? With Buddhism, this seems to be the belief in karma. I don't know how the beliefs in karma differ between various schools–Pure Land, Tibetan, Zen, etc.

I find the whole belief in karma to be very, very difficult to accept. It seems like logic is thrown out the window.

My experience is whenever you question karma, the response is either "ask a more educated guru" or "you aren't ready to understand yet, keep trying." These responses, to me, still means it's a leap of faith no matter how you look at it.

Karma: it's important to know what it is, and what it's not.

The Buddha's teaching is all about experience. He encourages us to question doctrine and authority. If we engage ideas—especially his—and they don't conform to our experience, we should reject them.

So, if we cannot confirm karma through experience, we should reject it.

Good Karma?

One reason karma is so difficult to understand is because it's a loaded term. What is karma? Is it luck? Is it the accumulation of deeds over millions of lifetimes? Does it mean "what goes around comes around?" Does it imply reincarnation?

Let's start at the beginning. Karma means action or the results of those actions. Perhaps the best way to look at karma is as cause and effect. It's *experience* in and of itself.

When I was three, I put my hand on a hot stove. It burned. For me, this was such a strong experience, it evoked my first word: hot. I also never touched a hot stove again.

Connecting our behavior to its consequences is how we learn. Karma teaches us to avoid hot stoves, to be kind to others, pay our bills, etc. Understanding karma is to understand that actions have consequences.

Where Do We Go From Here?

We respond to karma from the moment of birth. Crying gets our parents attention. Studying brings good grades and praise—lying leads to trouble.

Our relationship to karma is compelling. Learning is the skill that allows us to repeat behaviors that produce good karma. We're hooked on it. It's how we achieve success and happiness.

...Or is it?

There Lies the Rub

Does contentment arise from karmic success? The Buddha suggested that that's not the whole enchilada.

This is where the real learning starts: I like to think of it in terms of a baseball player's batting average. A great baseball player gets on base about 1/3 of the time. That's a poor ratio of success to failure, but it's considered respectable performance.

Now look at personal experience. Consider the correlation between our intentions, actions, and things turning out our way. What's your batting average? To me the phrase, "The road to hell is paved with good intentions," comes to mind. If we're honest with ourselves we'll recognize that we probably bat about .250 or .300.

Now...close your eyes. Take a moment to focus your awareness on your breath.

Count as each breath comes and goes. Keep going until you reach ten, or even better, thirty!

How do you feel? More relaxed? More focused? Perhaps you feel less anxious than you did before. You might even cede that for a brief moment you felt contentment.

What's important to recognize is that your effort was not directed towards achieving anything in particular. In fact you "accomplished" nothing. You just stepped out of the way of karma. By doing so, you've discovered your natural source of contentment.

You might think of meditation as an experiment with karma. When we sit with ourselves, we encounter monkey mind. Monkey mind is the operator of our karmic "mobile devices"—our bodies and minds.

Monkey mind is always moving on to the next thing. It's a karma junky, driven by the next pleasure. It never stops to savor the present pleasure.

As we discover in meditation, this monkey has a one track mind. If we aren't mindful of the power the monkey holds over us, it will drag us down.

What's the secret?

Our relationship to karma is critical to happiness. Success is tied up in it. If you make good decisions and act on them, your batting average will improve. Study hard, you can get good grades. Work hard, maybe you'll advance your career. Act with kindness and you can enjoy better relationships with others.

But we also have to remember batting .300 is awesome. There are many things outside of our control and bad things happen to good people.

We also have to remember that karma is not the source of contentment. Enlightenment is not batting 1000. We're going to strikeout. If we can't be happy with batting .300, we won't be happy.

Does Karma Matter?

Yes, karma matters. It provides the causes and conditions of happiness. For instance, financial security can allow you the time to have a regular spiritual practice. Having the time to meditate is important.

Meditation, being here and now, allows us to see the monkey mind for what it is. We shouldn't reject it. It is part of us. But know that it is only a single dimension of who we are.

In meditation, we discover our natural propensity for contentment. Being in the present moment is deeply satisfying without striving or manipulation. This dimension is the wellspring of happiness.

These two dimensions of karma and contentment are intertwined inextricably. Our karma, the result of our actions, is ours. Our inherent natural capacity for contentment is also ours. In a healthy state, these are in balance. Out of balance, we suffer.

If we are to strive towards anything, we should strive for balance; to be our whole selves, to be contented monkeys.

13 Karma Computing

Question on karma: *I feel there is no way around it. Karma assumes there is a system that tracks merit, transforms it into physical traits, the mood of our environment, our general health, etc. There must be a formula for transformation that tracks things like how many ants I squished as child is directly, or conversely, related to how compassionate I am now to friends, etc. There must be a super computer crunching values continuously for so many beings. Is there?*

Before I talk about "karma computing," I want to lay out some important ground work in the Buddhist teachings in the form of the three Dharma Seals, the parable of the arrow, and the Sutra of Totality.

The Three Dharma Seals

The Dharma seals are a litmus test. If a teaching contradicts any of these notions or makes claims beyond these fundamentals, it should be considered suspect and questioned. They are as follows:

Impermanence. Everything that has a beginning has an end.

Not self. We are impermanent; the notion of a permanent individual self is a delusion.

Nirvana. Freedom from the suffering that comes from the delusion of self. Nirvana is found in the balance, the yin and yang of self/non-self.

The Parable of the Arrow

"It's just as if a man were wounded with an arrow thickly smeared with poison. His friends & companions, kinsmen & relatives would provide him with a surgeon, and the man would say, 'I won't have this arrow removed until I know whether the man who wounded me was a noble warrior, a priest, a merchant, or a worker.' He would say, 'I won't have this arrow removed until I know the given name & clan name of the man who wounded me...until I know whether he was tall, medium, or short... until I know whether he was dark, ruddy-brown, or golden-colored... until I know his home village, town, or city...until I know whether the bow with which I was wounded was a long bow or a crossbow...until I know whether the bowstring with which I was wounded was fiber, bamboo threads, sinew, hemp, or bark...until I know whether the shaft with which I was wounded was wild or cultivated...until I know whether the feathers of the shaft with which I was wounded were those of a vulture, a stork, a hawk, a peacock, or another bird...until I know whether the shaft with which I was wounded was bound with the sinew of an ox, a water buffalo, a langur, or a monkey.' He would say, 'I won't have this arrow removed until I know whether the shaft with which I was wounded was that of a common arrow, a curved arrow, a barbed, a calf-toothed, or an oleander arrow.' The man would die and those things would still remain unknown to him."

Cula-Malunkyovada Sutta

The Sutra of Totality

Monks, I will teach you the totality of life. Listen, attend carefully to it and I will speak.

What, monks, is totality?

It is just the eye with the objects of sight; the ear with the objects of hearing; the nose with the objects of smell; the tongue with the objects of taste; the body with the objects of touch; and the mind with the objects of cognition. This, monks, is called totality.

Now, if anyone were to say, "Aside from this explanation of totality, I will preach another totality," that person would be speaking empty words, and being questioned would not be able to answer. Why is this? Because that person is talking about something outside of all possible knowledge.

Control

My day job is working as a program director for a fast growing oncology lab startup company. Each day is hard. Each day there are difficult problems to solve and important progress to be made. In a very real and tangible sense, my success or failure might impact the life of a person suffering from cancer.

There is a lot to absorb, and a lot to keep track of. My ability to focus on the right things at the right time is important. If I lose focus or get lost in the weeds, things fall apart quickly.

I think what's been helpful for me is recognizing the delusion of control. The delusion has two parts or two extremes. One: I have complete control over anything. Two: when I don't have control, someone else is in control.

Plans

"Life is what happens to you while you're busy making other plans."

Allen Saunders/John Lennon

Managing projects is about making plans and doing your darndest to stick to them. You need to deliver the product the customer wants by the date they've requested. The life of a project manager's is rarely smooth. They often meet with failure. Invariably, life gets in the way.

Why do plans fail?

Say your project is manufacturing a toaster. You have a supplier who is building a new heating element that will make your toaster the best on the market. But you discover that the supplier will be late delivering the part. You're going to be late to market and disappoint your investors.

Think about the last time you were late for work. What happened there?

In your mental list of what could have happened, was there a supercomputer crunching out karmic consequences? No, the causes were much less mysterious. The toaster project was probably impacted by a manufacturing glitch. You were probably late for work because you forgot to set the alarm clock or hit the snooze button too many times. These are the causes.

The Sutra of Totality reminds us that we can only rely on what we perceive with our senses. *Why is it we introduce concepts beyond perception to explain things?* What is it that leads you to the assumption that there is something like a supercomputer crunching out karma?

Poison

"The riddles of God are more satisfying than the solutions of man."

G. K. Chesterton

I think there are compelling reasons to consider mystical ideas, but we need to be careful how we apply them.

The Parable of the Arrow reminds us what's important. Recognizing that we've been poisoned by the arrow leads us to the obvious solution—seek treatment. Knowing *why* consequences follow actions offers no advantage.

Does invoking a karmic deity offer you any help dealing with the delay in your project? Can you blame a karmic supercomputer for making you late for work? It's utterly unhelpful.

It's the delusion of control. The notions that a mystical super computer exerts control or that we are in control are diversions.

It works like this. We adjust our schedule to work around the delay. We remember to set our alarm clock the next day. But we also know that life gets in the way. It's something that we recognize and act on every day without a second thought.

Karma Computing

I have to admit, your question concerned me. It made me think that you'd received a Buddhist teaching that implied or explicitly claimed that Karma is controlled in some way by a Buddha (or a supercomputer). I see no evidence for that. Continue to ask questions and seek clarity on karma and other Dharma concepts. But remember this: a good life is not found seeking answers to unanswerable questions.

14 Politics—Another Word For Disappointment?

Question: *From a Buddhist standpoint, could you give your opinion on some political issues of your choosing?*

The Buddha actually offered advice in the arena of politics and government. There are teaching related to politics, including the Dasa Rája Dharma and the story of Ummadayantí.

Politics can be a cause of heartburn. If this is the case for you, take a step back for a moment and examine the source of your dissatisfaction.

With politics and other issues that are subject to such strong polarity, the most helpful teaching that Buddhism offers is the Madyamaka, or the Middle Way.

The Spectacle

It's not hard to see—especially during a presidential election—that the American political process is a bit of a circus. Liberals and conservatives at the extreme ends of the spectrum shape political conversations through absurdly simple sound bites. If we adopt election year rhetoric—hook, line, and sinker—we deserve what we get.

The Middle Way

The story of the Siddhartha Gautama's enlightenment is the story of the Middle Way.

For a long time before the Buddha, the concept of dissatisfaction was well understood in India. It was a fundamental premise of the ancient yogic tradition.

Dissatisfaction, or dukka, was diagnosed as an attachment to a preferred future. The equation is simple. We want things to turn out one way, and if they don't, we're left dissatisfied.

The remedy for attachment was austerity. Yogis would strive to overcome their desires by doing without. These ascetics are well-known for their vows of homelessness, starvation, and severe physical hardships.

The Buddha excelled at austerity, surpassing all of his teachers. But he failed to reach Nirvana. He failed and he nearly died trying to achieve it.

His choice of austerity was a response to his upbringing. As a child he was raised in opulence. A prince and a member of the warrior class, he wanted for nothing. Yet in his late twenties, even after the birth of his son, he was still unsatisfied.

Neither comfort nor austerity led him to contentment. Both paths failed. Satisfaction, he ultimately discovered, came from somewhere else.

Austerity vs. Comfort

If we stop for a moment, we'll recognize the parallel between the Buddha's two failed paths and the two ends of the American political spectrum.

Consider the Great Recession. In the last decade, our nation was in the worst economic crisis since the Great Depression. Two political options were presented: Conservatives offered austerity. Liberals offered spending to maintain our standard of living.

The Buddha's choices–austerity and comfort–mirror our political choices today…and he chose neither. It seems that the response to politics should be the same—neither. Wake up!

Attachment

When we become attached to an ideology, it will eventually become a source of suffering.

I remember when George W. Bush was reelected; the liberal world erupted with a bitter campaign of disrespect. Photos of people holding up signs saying "we're sorry" appeared all over the net. Conservatives were angered.

It's interesting how the preference for a candidate and their message can have such power over us. It's actually disconcerting. The causes of history's great tragedies are less about leaders, and more about the people who are willing to follow them.

Hitler would not have achieved the power he did, if the majority of Germans didn't accept his methods and politics. Stalin, Pol Pot, and Mao required the acquiescence of huge numbers of people to carry out their evil.

In politics, attachment and even worse, allegiance to an ideology can lead to disaster. It can blind us to the truth of what is really going on. But consider the alternative—complete disengagement. If we exit from politics and give up entirely, we are subject to the same suffering. The other contributing factor to the disaster of utopian regimes like Hitler's Third Reich is that people abdicated their moral responsibilities. These people are equally at fault.

Both attachment and disengagement are forms of blindness that lead to suffering.

It's Complicated

For every complex problem there is an answer that is clear, simple, and wrong.

H. L. Mencken

In many ways, elections are a referendum on the economy. Candidates run based on their party's economic formula. They insist with confidence that their solutions will prevail. Yet, the complexity of the economy is such that people who dedicate their lives to the science are quick to state the inadequacy of their understanding. It's complicated. The certainty with which politician's claim to predict the future is staggering in the face of the truth.

In my opinion, the founding fathers applied great insight and forethought to protect us from the delusions of politics. The structure of our government, with its checks and balances, protects us from those who profess clear and simple ideological solutions. The dysfunction of government is in one sense a blessing—albeit an expensive one.

Political Opinions

With these points in mind, my political opinions tend to be cautionary, rather than in favor of a particular ideology.

Politics are important and, yes, I do have political preferences, and you should too, but make an effort to see them in the context of the circumstances. In order to prevent the tragedies of the past, we have to take the political process seriously. We must engage it with a clear and disciplined mind.

Our civic and religious freedoms are precious. If we are not diligent in protecting them we have only ourselves to blame. Political extremism, allegiances to ideologies, and being disengaged are the symptoms of attachment and aversion. These symptoms of blindness leave us vulnerable to tyranny.

This country's greatness is captured in its Constitution. It limits the power of government. It gives us the power to prevent tyranny. But we must be its guardians. We must be awake to the task.

A Buddha is an awakened being, free from delusions. The path of the Buddha prepares us to be awake to all of life, including the task of governing ourselves.

15 Darwin's Dharma

They say that death comes suddenly and without warning. But nothing could be further from the truth. There is no doubt about our mortality. Yet we live our lives like we're oblivious to it.

The easy take away from this realization is *carpe diem*. Live today like it's your last. It's logically obvious.

But logic doesn't govern the human psyche. We are decidedly not Vulcans. In fact, even when we're given enough information about our situation, we often still manage to make bad choices. (I'm not trying to depress you. In fact, I'm trying to do the opposite.)

Jvala Pravataya Hum

At the beginning of every Sangha sitting, I recite a Light Mantra. *Om Amogha Amitabha Mahámudra Mani Padma Jvála Pravarttaya Húm*. The word *Pravarttaya* can be translated as evolve. *Jvala* means light. I have been taught that we can take this as an indication that the world is evolving toward the light. Things are getting better all the time.

Evolution

The theory of evolution is still teaching us. Some of the brightest minds in the world are discovering applications for the theory far beyond what Charles Darwin may have imagined. In the field of artificial intelligence, Ray Kurzweil has been using "evolutionary systems" to generate superior designs. It's done using the same process of random mutation and natural selection.

By creating a baseline design, subjecting it to random permutations, and testing it in competition with other "mutant" designs, Kurzweil has produced amazing results. The failed designs "die off," and the better designs go on to give birth to future design generations.

With the incredible processing power of today's computers, Kurzweil is able to simulate the millions of generations it takes to "evolve" a species by compressing the generations into nanoseconds.

Through massive failure—because, after all, most designs fail—these evolutionary systems can produce better quality more efficiently and more effectively than "intelligent" human designers.

Why So Negative?

Massive Failure = Success! It's a puzzling equation, but the evidence is powerful when you examine experience. Still, it seems so...negative.

Buddhism is often accused of being negative. Is it? Yes and No. I appreciate Buddhism because it's very scientific. The Buddha connects with us on very personal and pragmatic terms. He does it by bringing attention to the data about our failures and the value these data hold for us.

We are all consciously, or unconsciously, seeking to answer the question, "What's missing in my life?" If we're fortunate, we're conscious of this void and we rationally seek to fill it. We might take on a spiritual practice, a hobby, or a purpose in life. But more often than not, we spend our lives trying to fill the void with food, cigarettes, alcohol, technology, shopping, the list goes on. These are our cravings and addictions. But the cravings are never satisfied.

This is the failure that the Buddha was talking about. We're oblivious to the data that tells us we're not succeeding.

Of course, he reminds us, there is "good news." He tells us there's a way out of the vicious cycle.

Can We Learn From Our Failures?

"Even if one escapes from the evil creations, it is one's rare fortune to be born as a human being. Even if he be perfect in all the six senses, it is his rare fortune to be born in the middle kingdom. Even if he be born in the middle kingdom, it is his rare fortune to be born in the time of a Buddha. Even if he be born in the time of a Buddha, it is his rare fortune to see the enlightened. Even if he be able to see the enlightened, it is his rare fortune to have his heart awakened in faith. Even if he has faith, it is his rare fortune to awaken the heart of intelligence. Even if he awakens the heart of intelligence, it is his rare fortune to realize a spiritual state which is above discipline and attainment."

The Buddha

It is a great fortune to be human in the 21st century. The comforts available to us—the accessibility to medicine and technology—all provide us with an extremely high quality of life. Our cognitive faculties give us the ability to reflect on our lives and seek ways to improve our lot. We have amazing thinking tools like logic and the scientific method. Computers can perform massive amounts of number crunching that allow us to model and solve problems.

It's like we've won the lottery! Yet somehow we find ways to see our situation as hopeless. We don't respond well to admonitions like, "we've got it great," and "why can't we be happy." As I said earlier, logic doesn't rule the human psyche.

"Knowledge rests not upon truth alone, but upon error also."

Carl Jung

If there is a message we can take from evolution, it's that failure is the engine that drives success. Most mutations result in abysmal failure and often death. But once in a great while, an alteration in the genetic code yields slight advantages that increase the likelihood that the organism will successfully reproduce.

Perhaps the Buddhist analogy to this is the great fortune of being born human. In this life we have the capacity to achieve enlightenment. But in the Buddha's formulation of the odds, there is still a great distance to cover between the luck of being born human...and liberation. Without awakening the heart of intelligence, we are doomed to the cyclical life of Samsara.

The Buddha reflects on our failures and demands that we reckon with them. He prods us to look at our patterns of behavior and acknowledge that they often do more damage than good. It takes deep reflection on our circumstances to awaken our hearts. But in that reflection, if we can clearly see the great engine of failure that drives Samsara, we can be inspired to transform.

Like I said, I'm not trying to depress you. I hope to inspire you.

If we meditate on our experience, reflect on the data, we should recognize some of the salient patterns and truths. Death is sure to come. Filling the void with addictions perpetuates suffering. These truths are loud and clear if we are awake enough to see them.

If our equation (Massive Failure = Success) has anything to offer, it's that we have enough evidence to support a resolution to transform. We should live our lives as if today will be our last. We should be working towards kindness, compassion, joy, and equanimity. We should meditate regularly to reinforce the notion that being fully in the present moment is the only source of lasting contentment.

Don't just do something, sit!

16 The Messenger and the Message

Question: *Looking at other religions, do you find them at all lacking? If so, how?*

I believe all religions are rightfully subject to criticism. They're human institutions that can fall prey to corruption and the foibles of human nature. But, rather than criticize other religions, I find it better to look to Buddhism's faults and generalize how these faults are usually shared across all religions.

A story I often tell to people who come to Buddhism out of aversion to their birth religion is about my first visit to Asia. I was traveling on business to Tokyo, and I was very excited on several levels. I was going to a new place with new things to learn and see. But most of all, I was intrigued by the fact that I would be in a country in which Buddhism was a near majority religion.

I would get to see how much better, spiritually speaking, things would be! Oh, how I was wrong! On several levels I was disappointed. On my first visit to a Buddhist place of worship, I was reminded of the story of Jesus and his encounter with the money changers outside the Temple in Jerusalem.

The temple was the center of a tourist trap surrounded by vendors selling souvenirs and various religious knick-knacks. The temple itself was an elaborate wishing well where you could purchase blessings from a priest and make "auspicious" contributions. It was elaborate, ornate, and worldly in a way that made me wonder if Japanese Buddhists had even considered the Buddha's admonishment about attachment!

My own path to Buddhism grew out of an aversion to Christianity. The stark differences I saw between Christ and the religion founded in his name alienated me. My disappointment was deep when I came to realize that the Buddha and Buddhism are also two very different beasts.

Unfortunately, religions are almost inevitably corrupted. They become organizations that strive to acquire and maintain power. As a result, they diverge in purpose and suffer from serving two masters.

The Buddha didn't teach about how to construct and perpetuate organizations. He didn't provide instruction on how to accumulate power. These functions arise out of a mix of good intentions and delusion.

But there is a benefit to this uneasy symbiosis. It's a fact that Buddhism relies on the power of the Buddha's message to survive. Conversely, the teachings are available to us today because of the institution of Buddhism.

Religions are easy targets for criticism. But if you look to their core you'll discover their true message. Buddhism tells us that the journey is inward and that the teachings are but a raft to reach the other side. When the raft has served its purpose, it is no longer of use and can be set aside.

Acknowledging the weaknesses of religion is important to protect yourself from its dark side. You should be quick to cast aside dogma that only serve to maintain institutional status quo.

Look for the heart of a tradition in the actions of its humble servants and selfless teachers. Listen and let the teachings be borne out, or set aside, based on your experience.

Remember that religious institutions carry in them great pearls. The Vedas, the Torah, and the Tao all hold kernels of wisdom that can enrich our lives. They encapsulate the memory and insight of our ancestors. They are an offering wrapped in unconditional love that's gifted directly to you.

17 Get Down With Your Bad Self

If you're a fan of funk music (and you're as old as I am), you've probably shaken your hips to the sounds of James Brown, Parliament, Sly and the Family Stone, Kool and The Gang, or Tower of Power.

Funk is liberating. You cast off your inhibitions; embrace your bad self and open up. In the words of George Clinton, free your mind and your ass will follow. There's some truth to that.

Get up offa that thing

And shake till you feel better.

Get up offa that thing

And try to release that pressure.

James Brown

The Buddha's teaching is about embracing our entire being, our full potential. This is accomplished by way of bridging the gaps between others and ourselves.

Alienation and anxiety arise when we don't embrace our full potential. They are the symptoms of a fractured relationship with the world. In yogic terms, this fractured view is called avidya. *Avidya* means not seeing. It is blindness to our true potential.

The Great Embrace

We are all two sided coins. On one side, we are independent and reliant upon our wits to survive and thrive. On the other, we are completely dependent upon others. Striving for independence is necessary, especially early in life. We must be taught to care for ourselves and develop our individual talents. We learn to become self-reliant.

This *self*-conditioning is reinforced into adulthood, especially in this age of individualism. As individuals, we are alone.

But we are also part of a whole. We are interconnected with the people and environment around us. We share the energy and experience of others. We are in touch with them in ways that transcend individuality.

Unfortunately, we're easily disconnected from the world. This split personality disorder is revealed to us as dis-ease. When we're out of balance, we suffer from physical and mental illness. Health, from the Old English, is literally wholeness.

What's Funk Got to Do with It?

I frequently need to be reminded by loved ones that I get caught up in the "doing" of the independent self. I am quick to fall out of balance. I get mindlessly absorbed in accomplishing things in my roles as a father, a worker, and a teacher. So much so, that I become disconnected from my family, friends, and even the space around me. When this happens, I often end up in a funk.

Ironically, funk embraces both ends of the spectrum. On one side funk music is uplifting. But being *in a funk* is the dark side of our emotional self. So, if we're to embrace our entire being, how do we embrace the dark side?

The Hellenic tradition has a particularly poignant icon for the dark side. Hekate is the goddess of the underworld. Carl Jung describes her as the shadow self. Her invocation is dark, but it beckons us to reconnect:

I am the darkness that covers this broken, tortured land.

I bring the stillness, the quiet, the pause.

I am the healing, the regeneration, for the new dawn to reveal.

I am the Goddess of Death,

And I am one with you.

In you, Of you, Around you, I am you, And you are me.

I am here, always, with you.

For you are mine, as I am yours.

Eternally.

What does the darkness have to say? When I'm in a funk, I withdraw. I turn inward and away from others. Hekate is leading me to the stillness, the quiet, and the pause.

She is the Goddess of darkness, but she's depicted as holding a torch. She is the companion of Hades, but the minister of the Goddess of Spring, Persephone. She represents the night—the time of sleep and regeneration. She is the Goddess of the crossroads, those defining points in life where we wake up and choose a different path. She reminds us that the night leads to day, to wholeness and rebirth.

Hekate is urging us to be mindful in the darkness, holding the light to it. How else do we take the first step to recovery when we lose our way? We must acknowledge it—everything from admitting addiction to recognizing the symptoms of depression—we must be aware of it. Mindfulness lies at the threshold of wholeness, health, and happiness.

The funk of darkness carries all of her messages. She reminds us to take time to rest and regenerate, to reconnect with others, and to reach out for help. But if we aren't listening, what can be done? Hekate rings the door bell, but we have to be home to answer.

Disco Inferno

From a Buddhist perspective, this need to wake up, to reach out and ask for help, is called relying on Other Power. The path of faith and vows tells us that we cannot rely on self-power for salvation.

Beyond self-power, beyond our cocoon of ego and avidya, lies freedom from addiction, mindlessness, and suffering. From the shadows comes Hekate with the torch. She urges us to wake up, reach out, and reconnect with others. Mindfulness in the stillness, the quiet, the pause hearkens us back to health.

When we chant the name of the Buddha, we are affirming our reliance on others. We are calling out for the light of Hekate's torch to show us the way.

As I grow older and a little more experienced with the nature of my *self*, I am reminded that having a conceptual understanding of wholeness is not enough. Practicing what I preach is more important.

This is real life. It's kind of like a high school dance. We're full of nerves and anticipation. Calling to Buddha Amitabha is like asking for the first dance. It takes presence, courage, and wherewithal to step beyond the small self out onto the dance floor and into the arms of someone else. But experience tells us that the connection is worth it.

There is something to be said for getting on the dance floor of life. Move around in the darkness. Get up offa that thing and shake 'til you feel better. Move around in the space of your relationships and slow dance in the silence of being with others. Dance, connect, and live.

18 Putting It Off

It's a Guild cutaway acoustic guitar with Fishman pickups. It has an onboard tuner and EQ. The sound is big and so is the price tag. The running joke whenever I walk into a guitar shop is, "I'm just going in to get some strings…oh, and they might have a guitar attached." I imagine all the things that I could do with it. If only I had that guitar.

And so for all of us, this is the search for happiness. Our desire to scratch the itch. If I save my money and get the Guild, then I'll be happy. The trouble is, I already have a beautiful guitar. Not as nice as the one I'm dreaming of, but wonderful just the same.

What drives us to hitch our happiness to the future? When I pine for the guitar, I seem to be saying, "I'm not content right now, but when I get it, boy will I be happy." I end up driving a wedge between happiness and now.

Getting Through the Grind

I remember my first job. I was a paperboy. I delivered the Hartford Courant in my neighborhood. I'd be up at 5:00 a.m. on my bike through winter and summer. The memories are vivid. It was a struggle every day to get out of bed, especially on cold winter mornings. The mindset I adopted was to tell myself to, "just get through this," for there'd will be better days.

We apply this strategy to all aspects of life, get through the grind now—enjoy later. I coped with school, work, and lots of other parts of my life this way. I learned to put it off. It being life.

Living in Our Own Future

What's ironic is that we're living in the moments that we planned for in the distant and not so distant past. If we look around we have many of the possessions, relationships, and comforts that we hoped for not so long ago. The time to be happy is now.

Sometimes we have to plan for the future. It's the responsible thing to do. But remember that planning you did yesterday? Yes, well, take some time out to enjoy the fruits of that labor. Be in the moment; be in your relationships, and most of all take time to abide.

So sit down at the piano, or grab your clarinet, or sing that song. Grab some friends and play it together. There is so much joy to be had, don't put it off.

19 Nature's Rhythms

Recently, I had a pretty nasty stomach bug. To put it politely, my body hadn't worked that hard to expel its contents in a long time. Leave it to me to find a teachable moment while retching.

It's amazing how the body takes care of itself. While there was no pleasure in the way my body cured itself, I wondered at its efficiency.

This is how we are. We come to balance effortlessly. All we have to do is get out of the way.

The Hindus have a metaphor for the uniformity of nature called Indra's Net. It is an infinite matrix of interconnected gems, each jewel perfectly reflecting all the others. It illustrates the idea that the macrocosm is reflected in the microcosm. Within each of us is all the mystery and order of the universe.

On one hand this seems obvious; we are all made of the stuff of stars. But in our day-to-day lives, we fall prey to notions that somehow we are different, that we need to fix something about ourselves to regain balance.

The natural order of things is embedded in our bodies and our minds. We can find peace by simply returning to the rhythms of nature.

As my stomach bug proved, my body is always self-adjusting towards balance.

It did what it needed to do. It got a virus, it expelled it. No pomp (or dignity) necessary, just expediency. It sent a clear message; I was sick. My job was to listen and take the time to heal.

Life is the up and down rhythms of sickness and health, joy and sadness. Amitabha Buddha is the personification of this never-ending pulse of life.

We can feel the natural rhythms in our daily lives and at the scale of the cosmos. While it may show up as temporary discomfort, things move to equilibrium.

Trusting in nature's rhythms is called taking refuge. Meditation is the practice of finding the rhythm within. Rest in your Buddha Nature a little every day. Remember that what needs to be done is done. Listen closely to your body, it will whisper the secrets of the cosmos.

20 Purr-spective

She was black, with a white bib and white paws. A gentle, friendly cat, Annabelle stood in sharp contrast to the cats that came before her.

My first childhood cats, Smokey and Dum Dum, had been the brutish neighborhood strays, battle scarred and fairly indifferent to human attention. Annabelle was different. We connected.

As a boy, my first real prayers were for her. She had gone missing for almost a week. In tears, I made my pleas to God. When she returned, my relief was complete.

But after that, He vanished from my life—no longer urgently needed. Such is our relationship with God.

What's with the God Talk?

As a Buddhist, when I talk about *God*, I want to be careful to define my terms. I'm not implying proof of Her (or Him) existence. I'm using the term in the familiar way, based on usage, not facts. We all use the word casually. So much so that it's well understood by everyone—independent of the real meaning. Even atheists have a place in their lexicon for the word God.

What I find useful about the word God is that it is a placeholder for something we could consider sacred. However poorly defined the sacred might be, it seems to strike a chord, dissonant or harmonious, with everyone.

What is our relationship to God?

If we have one, our relationship with God is intensely private. We don't relate to him in the same way we do with a cat or a friend. The connection is different. And it's often distant.

I've participated in several Lakota sweat lodges. Early in the day, the leader asks what prayers we have. His role in the ceremony is to act as an intercessor, to speak for the Grandfathers in response to our prayers.

The experience underscores the peculiarity of our relationship with the divine. Most of us don't know what it means to have one. Those who have one, easily lose sight of it. So easily that we rely on others to broker it for us. Being with God is slippery.

50,000-Foot View

When I prayed for Annabelle, I was looking for someone to bring my cat back. Is that what God is—a pet retrieval service? I don't think so. When we talk about how God is in the world, we have to recognize that She doesn't just walk down the street. We have to speak in metaphors. She eludes concrete definition.

I think we have to set aside the desire to understand God.

But we can try to ask different questions, like; what is the role that God plays in our lives?

I suggest one way is in offering perspective.

Not to be presumptuous, but what is God's perspective? Trying to imagine what this means is an opportunity to crack the shell of our ego. What happens when we expand our outlook to consider a wider view, one that transcends our own interest and includes other people, our community and our environment?

If we could set our egos aside, wouldn't we be more capable of justice? If we could see our desires in the context of others, wouldn't we be more capable of compassion? If we could see our competition for status as self-defeating, wouldn't we be more capable of contentment?

If we were to make an effort to move in the direction of God, these virtues would only increase. Of course, we can't possibly take on the perspective of God. But isn't it worthwhile moving in that direction?

Get Real

The Buddha's great insight was that this is the only real perspective. The perspective of *me* is limiting and produces suffering. When we move towards the perspective of the Buddha, we naturally uncover great virtues and great happiness.

Ironically, not long after she returned home, Annabelle was hit by a car. This time she wasn't coming back. But I really cherished the time I had left with her. Perspective gave me the nudge I needed to appreciate that most things in life are temporary and precious.

By moving closer to Buddha, great compassion, wisdom, and bliss become available to us. In the sense that we are all capable of this, the Buddha, the sacred, lies within each of us.

21 Being Angry

I recently saw a quote on Twitter that struck me:

When anger rises remember compassion.

It's one of those sound bites that tug my strings. When I'm angry, how can I be compassionate? I'm too busy being angry. If, as the Buddhist teachings imply, I'm perfect the way I am, why do I need to act differently?

I was reminded of another quote from Suzuki-Roshi:

"All of you are perfect just as you are, and you could use a little improvement."
Shunryu Suzuki

Buddhist sound bites can seem like double speak. Can we feel anger and compassion at the same time? You'd think no.

Losing Our Minds

For many years, I worked in the mental health industry caring for people with severe behavior disorders. Sometimes I would need to use restraints to prevent them from doing harm to themselves or others.

Part of my training was learning when and how to apply safe restraint techniques. The most important tool in the toolbox was the ability to gauge rationality.

Violent behavior is typically preceded by a loss of rationality and it's associated with the hormone adrenaline. When adrenaline kicks in, our ability to reason is all but lost.

Adrenaline prepares us for fight or flight. It causes our bodies to react differently. We become faster and stronger, but we become mentally inflexible. Humans are hardwired for irrationality when we feel cornered.

What does it mean for us to be cornered? As soon as we feel that the situation is out of our control, anxiety sets in, and the adrenaline takes effect.

The Antidote

I think you can look at the problem of anxiety from two angles. The first is recognizing the things in our environment that make us feel threatened. The other is grappling with the concept of control.

Of course, we can do our best to avoid situations where we feel threatened, but we often have little control over our circumstances. If we're looking for an effective antidote to anxiety, we should look at our ideas about control. If we have any power at all, it is over our ideas.

The delusion of control is powerful. When things fall apart, our level of anxiety is directly proportional to the degree to which we're deluded.

How Big Are Our Corners?

Here's an example. Think about setting your alarm clock. All you need to do is set the time and turn the alarm on. If you did everything right, you'll be up on time the next morning. You're in complete control, right?

Nothing could be further from the truth. You rely on a vast network of people and materials all outside of your control. You need the power company. You need the poles and wires to bring electricity into your home. You need a job to earn money to pay the electric bill, so on and so forth. In that vast network of interdependencies, any number of things could go wrong. None of which you can do anything about.

The notion that we are independent and self-reliant is extremely naïve. Any control that we think we have is limited. Acknowledging this can be difficult. In fact, it introduces anxiety. Coming to terms with our interdependence is very important.

From a Buddhist perspective, we have to have faith. But we don't just adopt faith; we have to come to recognize it. Faith and gratitude all come from the knowledge that we rely on others. Acknowledging our faith is taking refuge in the Buddha.

Getting Real

Mindfulness gives us the power to transform. When we open our eyes to the faith and reliance we have in others, we are naturally drawn toward gratitude. We also recognize that we have the support of our friends, community, and even complete strangers.

When we see interdependence clearly, the pressure eases. We can and do rely on others. Knowing others have our backs naturally decreases our tendency to respond defensively. Anger can still arise, but it arises in a larger space.

Compassion in Anger

Can compassion arise with anger? Not in our tiny corners. Not when we're deluded that we have control. We don't have the spaciousness to hold anger in compassion. But if we accept the spaciousness of our faith, when anger arises we can offer it up to the Buddha to hold for us. The Buddha is the ocean of all creation and can receive it effortlessly. When anger arises, remember the Buddha is there to hold it for you.

22 Anticipation

Christmas presents: Maybe it's a sign of my age, but my favorite part of Christmas as an adult has always been watching the faces of my kids opening that special gift that they'd been pining for all year. That explosive facial expression, the glimmer in the eye, and the nonsense words of gratitude are the high points of the Christmas season.

For most young American kids, there is no greater longing than for Christmas morning. I remember my sister and I would shiver with anticipation, eager to get those presents open.

I wonder what has passed from then to now. It's not a melancholy wondering, but the question that the season and age, eventually asks of you.

Innocence

When it comes to Buddhism, I've struggled with how to engage children and youth. Its tenants can be dry and logical. The message of the Buddha speaks to a certain amount of experience that most children are free of.

I empathize with the story of the Buddha's father. Legend has it he went through great effort to shelter young Siddhartha from witnessing sickness, old age, and death. Who's to say there is any benefit in impressing upon children the frailty of life? Children, of all people, are alive in the moment.

Indeed, there is something to learn from the openness of children. The immediacy of their pleasure and their emotional authenticity reveals a certain purity that's lacking in adults.

The Gift of Time

> If the doors of perception were cleansed, everything would appear as it is, infinite.
>
> William Blake, "The Marriage of Heaven & Hell"

Look at how, as adults, we've changed from youth. There is an age when we begin to long for the way Christmas used to feel. Compared to our youth, the quality of our experience seems diminished.

Of course, aging affects our senses, but there is a greater barrier to authentic experience. It is our conditioned mind. It is the weight the past places on the present moment.

The Gift of Life

There are two facets to life—our constantly unfolding experience, and being. While our experiences seem the most tangible, ironically they are the least "real,"—the Buddha hints that there is something more "real."

There are many allusions to this fundamental aspect of being: the infinite light of Amitabha; Buddha nature; Rigpa; etc. To get a little less abstract, let's call it unconditioned or non-dual awareness.

Together, these facets—experience and being—form who we are. When they're in balance, we can just *be*. Peace, spontaneity, and contentment arise naturally. We return to an almost childlike state. We can find these moments in meditation, in nature, or in flashes of clarity.

Balancing the Scales

The rich complexity of human experience is beautiful and awesome. It is the play of our memories, hopes, and circumstances. Our relationships, love, hate, and the whole spectrum of emotions are rooted in experience.

Buddhism encourages us to step back from the cacophony and sit. To be of practical value, we should understand the purpose of meditation. The goal is not to shelter ourselves from the experience of life. It is to recalibrate ourselves, to set the scales back to zero, so we can fully enjoy our lives.

Day after day, we accumulate road dust. We develop conditioned responses to the things we love, and the things we hate. As we adopt routines over spontaneity, the scales shift off of zero. We live less in the precious world of unfolding experience and more in our heads.

In meditation, we return to the natural equilibrium of being and experience. We are reacquainted with the child-like quality of experience. From this center we can recognize the weight of the world for what it is and gently remove it from our shoulders. From there, a balance is remembered and renewed.

Anticipation.

When we approach the holidays, we usually do it from an unbalanced perspective. Be it from dread or from great anticipation, our next moments can only fail to live up to our expectations.

Buddhism doesn't promise a better, brighter holiday season, but it encourages you to be there for the one you have. Understand the balance, the weight, and the anticipation. Notice the gifts along with the difficulties. Experience tells you that the good times make the hard times worth it. Don't miss being there for the good times.

23 The Trinity

One of the hats I wear in life is the role of a religious educator at my Unitarian Universalist church. I recently helped develop a curriculum for a 7th grade class called neighboring faiths. It gives the youth exposure to other faith traditions as they venture on their search for truth.

The approach I take to looking at other faith traditions is grounded in the yogic tradition. It all begins with introspection and works its way out. In the class, I have the youth look at faith traditions across three dimensions:

How does the faith tradition view the individual?

What does it hold to be sacred?

How does the faith tradition inform us about how to live in relationship to the world around us?

For instance, here is a highly simplified view of Christianity based on this approach:

- Individuals are created by God in his own image.

- Christians worship and receive the grace of God.

- God granted man dominion over the world.

By the nature of these relationships we can infer a great many things about how Christians might conduct themselves. In relationship to the creator, Christians would be indebted to and deeply grateful to God for the gift of life. In relationship to the world around them, Christians would be grateful for the bounties that sustain them. They would be obliged to foster good stewardship over creation. Each and every person, flower, animal, and mineral contributes to our well-being and can be viewed as a gift from God.

In this respect Christianity's view of the world is highly consistent with Buddhism. In fact it would be difficult to find any religion that, when viewed through this prism, would contradict these principles of relationship. The particulars of what is defined as sacred will be different, one God, many Gods, no God, but the outcomes are the same.

24 Always Half Way There

Many years ago, I attended a weekend martial arts camp with my son and several good friends. One of the senior black belts was also a Presbyterian minister. He offered a Sunday service, which we attended. Coincidentally, his topic for the service was a comparison between Christianity and Buddhism. I don't think he was aware that there was a Buddhist in his flock.

He began his talk by asserting his credentials. He had studied comparative religion as part of his degree in divinity. Then he laid out some popular, albeit incorrect, assumptions about Buddhism and used them to make a case for Christianity's superiority. To someone who didn't understand Buddhism, the argument may have made complete sense.

If someone with a degree in divinity can misunderstand and misrepresent Buddhism, then what about the rest of us?

Half a Paradox

The Greek Philosopher Zeno left us with a number of interesting puzzles. One was called the dichotomy paradox. It stated that in order to reach a point B from point A, you have to travel half way, say to point C. Of course, to get to C, you have to travel half way to that point. This goes on ad nauseam. Since you have to go half way an infinite number of times, it is impossible to actually reach point B

The point that I wanted to take from this is that if you only go halfway, you'll never get there.

My Presbyterian friend argued that Buddhism leads its followers to the belief that nothing exists. He claimed that the Buddhist doctrine of emptiness is nihilistic. For him, then, it followed that Buddhism is inferior. It will lead its adherents to despair and away from salvation.

True, any religion that leads to the conclusion that nothing exists has to be absurd. If the Buddha taught this, then following the Buddha's teachings would be as foolish as believing Zeno's claim that you can't get there from here.

Nothing is Something

"Form is emptiness, emptiness is form."

The Heart Sutra

The foundation of his argument was the Buddhist concept of emptiness. This doctrine can be simultaneously liberating and frightening. It is important to fully grasp its meaning and its implications.

The great Buddhist saint Nagarjuna characterized sunyata, or emptiness, as a dangerous snake. If you don't know how to handle it, it will bite you. Taken out of context or in parts, it can be mistaken for nihilism.

One of the first realizations of Buddhism is that all things are impermanent and therefore empty of inherent existence.

Take a flower. It comes into being as a result of a seed, water, nutrients, sunlight, etc. It doesn't exist independent of the seed or the water. Without them, there would be no flower.

All objects in the world are empty of inherent existence. They do not exist independently of other things.

So far, there is nothing frightening about emptiness. It's consistent with common sense.

But when we apply this logic to ourselves, we are forced to recognize that we are also empty by nature. Our existence is completely dependent upon other phenomenon. We are made from the seeds of our parents. We are what we eat. We're a product of our upbringing and our circumstances. We can't point to anything that is purely, in and of itself, us.

Does this mean we don't exist? Yes and no.

Do we exist on our own, independent of other things? No.

Do we exist in the same way that a flower exists? Of course.

Why the distinction? Because it gives us clarity on our relationship to the world. We are not separate from our community or our environment. We are deeply connected to them. It reminds us that we are just like the flower. It gives us a sense of belonging.

Emptiness, Really? What Now?

Understanding this concept is an important step. But it's only the first step. The Buddha was very clear that we shouldn't take his word for it. We have to discover and verify (or contradict) what he had to say.

This is accomplished through self-examination, by being with ourselves. Yoga, Qigong, and meditation are different ways that we can apply mindfulness to test these ideas. It gives us the opportunity to experience the teachings.

By observing the nature of everything we are, we become more and more attuned to interdependence and impermanence. Our thoughts are not permanent. They don't exist, except in the context of other ideas or sensations. They arise, hold our attention briefly, and dissipate into nothingness. The sensations in our bodies change over time and are dependent on stimuli. Our bodies themselves are always changing. They grow, age, and ultimately cease functioning.

But these insights should not lead to despair. When carefully considered, impermanence and emptiness are really motivation for gratitude and mindfulness. Each and every moment is fleeting, a one of a kind event worth being there for.

Being in Emptiness

There is a great bliss to be found resting in emptiness. It frees you from the tension that the delusion of permanence creates. It's like the tension we feel when we try to hold something slippery in our hands, but it's felt throughout our entire being. Letting this go is deeply liberating.

Resting in emptiness, we develop a sense of equanimity that brings peace in the moment. The experience of resting in emptiness is deeply profound.

Being in Form

As we develop a deeper connection to emptiness. It permits us to live in proper perspective. The equanimity we find in meditation gives us the capacity to immerse ourselves in experience, both good and bad, without attachment or aversion.

When we learn that all phenomenon are empty, we can embrace life as a dancer, taking ever shifting and evolving form.

The miracle of Buddha Amitabha's pure light—our awareness—gifts us the ability to appreciate every precious moment.

Being All the Way There

So while emptiness without form is a bleak and terrible view. Emptiness as form and form as emptiness is cause to acknowledge the sacredness of all things. Buddhism sheds light on the holiness we seek.

I wish no ill will to my Presbyterian friend. Popular notions of Buddhism are rife with falsehoods. In the age of the internet, it is common for false ideas to become supporting data to a thesis. These are traps we all fall into.

I pray that he finds bliss in Christ, as I find it in the Buddha, the Dharma, and the Sangha. I also thank him for the clarity I've gained from the experience.

As Sergeant Esterhaus on *Hill Street Blues* used to say, *"Let's be careful out there."*

25 Buddhist Healing

When I first wandered into the Sangha that I lead today, it was to attend a special training on Buddhist Reiki. To be honest, I wasn't drawn in by the Reiki training itself, but more by the prospect of meeting a Buddhist Master. I was a hatha yoga practitioner, and I wanted to explore meditation deeper. It is a natural next step in the yogic path, and I wanted to meet a bona fide teacher.

Through my martial arts practice, I had a little experience with other eastern healing techniques, like shiatsu. It was just enough to be dangerous, but thus far, the techniques I'd learned had proven to be very helpful.

Generally though, healing practices weren't a big interest for me for a number of reasons. First, I didn't think I had the ability to take it on as a career. Second, there tended to be a lot of fluff tacked onto alternative healing techniques. That turned me off.

I've always been very skeptical about anyone who makes claims or uses methods that cannot be verified. Performing shiatsu massages for friends had a clear effect on them, and so to me there was evidence that it worked. But when someone mentions speaking with spirit guides, or something like that, I tune out fast.

So, while my new teacher offered a wonderful instruction on Reiki, I looked at the Reiki practice itself as just a vehicle for the Buddhist teaching. I kind of set it aside as less important.

The Ideal Buddhist

As years went by, my teacher would visit us and offer various other physical practices like Kai Gong. I deeply enjoyed the teachings but continued to separate out "the Buddhist teaching" from the physical practices. While I would do the physical practices, they held no priority for me, and I eventually lost interest in them.

There is a certain irony in this, having come from a long history of martial arts and yoga. But as I read and heard more Dharma, I became convinced that the physical aspects of the teachings were secondary to understanding concepts like emptiness and mind. It was as if the body was somehow disconnected from the truth.

Like many people starting down the path of Buddhism, I was drawn to certain popular notions. Having been a philosophy major in college, I was probably even more susceptible to developing a strong preference for the heady concepts of Buddhism.

With no shortage of books on the topic, I naturally chose titles and authors that fed into my particular slant. I was deeply enamored by impermanence and its implications. If this body is only temporary, how could physical activity have any bearing on truth with a capital T?

Armed with a clearer understanding of concepts like impermanence, attachment, and the true self from my Buddhist studies, I felt that I had come to a comfortable place with things. I'd *figured it out.*

Ice Pick to the Forehead

To my rescue, eventually and thankfully, came my teacher. He diagnosed my condition succinctly as "engineer mind." For me, it was just a matter of working out the equations. But equations are in the mind. If there is anything contrary to being in the here and now, it is being in a cloud of ideas, especially Buddhist ideas.

Embracing the physical aspects of the training has been illuminating. Over the course of a year or two, he offered us some yoga teachings. For me, the benefit is that they have taken my effort out of the clouds and into the here and now.

The different yogas are physical practices which bring awareness to the body. Using breath, postures, and the present moment, I am able to bear witness to the completed experience.

When I set aside the yoga and healing practices, I was rejecting one aspect of the truth in favor of another. I chose sides when both sides are required. If we're to be authentically alive, we must embrace everything experience has to offer, both through the body and the mind.

Answer the Call

Whether we pay attention to it or not, our mind and bodies are in sync. They often need to conspire to get us to listen. My personal experience has proven that my body has to do nothing short of screaming to get my attention.

In my mid-thirties, I was working sixty hours or more per week as a software engineer. I thought I could burn the candle at both ends. I had traded in taking care of my body for the opportunity to earn more money. Not long into the job, I came down with severe back spasms. Mind over matter didn't work. Being stuck in bed was the alarm going off for me.

These important moments in life give us a chance to listen and learn the lesson. If we have the wherewithal to see our own suffering, we have two opportunities. First, we can do something about a particular problem. I needed to take care of myself and balance my attention between work and life. Second, we can gain deep insight into our patterns of suffering.

I had the good fortune to follow the insight to the Buddha's way. I'm still learning and finding the balance. With it has come an increase in contentment and success. Paying attention and correctly self-diagnosing are fortunate capabilities. Many people go on suffering, physically and mentally, without any hope for insight or relief. Don't let the good fortune slip away. Stick to the dharma. Keep the faith in the Buddha's way; it has many great gifts to offer.

26 Reaching Out

I have a young friend who was seriously injured in a bike accident. He spent many weeks in ICU—and in a medically induced coma—while swelling on his brain slowly subsided. He's home now. His progress in many ways has been miraculous.

The experience was, of course, traumatic for his family and friends. But it has been inspiring to see how a community of people can form to align their intentions, energy, and effort for the sake of others.

The insight you get from observing a community create itself is remarkable. Our innate empathy has great power to bring us together and to heal.

A Facebook Page was created to allow friends and family to express their healing thoughts, prayers, and support. The outpouring was phenomenal. I did a regular healing prayer for him, and many on the site have reported doing the same. As the news trickled out about some of the successes in his recovery, I couldn't help but think that we may have done some good.

Health

The Buddha's teaching of the Four Noble Truths lays the ground work for healing. He described our condition the same way a doctor would. He gave a diagnosis (suffering). He identified the origins (the causes of suffering). He assured us that there is a way to restore health (cessation), and then prescribed a cure (the Eightfold Path).

When the Buddha suggested that the cause of suffering was the delusion that the conventional self was permanent, he nudged us to consider the truth about ourselves. When we define our "selves" by our physical characteristics, our roles, or our character, we are talking about transient things. There is nothing permanent about the small self.

But, you might object and say when we talk about "me," there is a sense of permanence. So the question might be, is there something lasting in the world that we can call "me"? What is that "me"?

The Whole Enchilada

The Pure Land path of realization begins with Buddha Amitabha. Amitabha is the Buddha of endless light and life. Amitabha is a metaphor for life and its gift of awareness.

Consider awareness. Is it lasting? Permanent? I don't know. It's tricky.

If we ask children to describe themselves, and then ask them the same question again at age forty, most of the answers will have changed. Does this mean that there is no such thing as me? Yes, and No. If we ask them whether they are the same person in the sense of "me-ness" they're likely to say, yes. By "me-ness," I mean the "thing" that has been watching the world throughout one's life. It might make sense to call that "me-ness" awareness.

Awareness is slippery. Pure awareness is not definable in the conventional sense. It's not any particular color. It doesn't have dimensions.

It's a conundrum. We can all agree that it is there. But we cannot point to it. It defies the subject-object perspective that we normally use to conceptualize our world. We cannot step back from our awareness and get a better perspective; it's an impossible task.

While it defies definition, it is an undeniable part of being. Along with the ephemeral machinery of living, they make an inseparable pair.

The Power of Amitabha

When we abide as a whole, for Buddhists this means meditation—we balance the transient and awareness. Out of this understanding we can form the basis of exploration into wholeness and how it is a healing truth.

For most of us, our patterns of consciousness are the barrier to wholeness. We dwell in the small and the temporary. We are gripped by these limiting views—republican, democrat; male, female; boss, subordinate. We form small conceptions based on these tiny dimensions. We can be blind to the vastness of others and ourselves.

This is what the Buddha called wrong view, or delusion. This is the cause of our suffering, our dis-ease.

But what if we were able to gradually decrease the effect of our mundane habits, thoughts, and views? What would be the healing power of wholeness?

The Buddha urged us to explore the possibilities through yoga and meditation.

Self-Healing

Traditions like yoga and Qigong are centered upon bringing us back to wholeness. How is this done? It is done by doing. It is done by *being* in the fullest possible sense.

When we do our Qigong exercises, we are bringing our body, breath, and mind together. We become acutely aware of the impact that awareness can bring to bear on our bodies. By bringing our attention to our body, we can relax and open up, releasing tension and allowing oxygen, nutrients, and immune agents to repair and renew.

These techniques also bring openness to the mind. We observe that preferences, aversion, and the need for control arise directly as tension in the body and on the breath. When we can free awareness from the constraints of small minded consciousness, there comes an immediate physical and mental release.

Health comes with wholeness.

The Boundaries of Awareness

Yoga and meditation are tools to bring self-healing through awareness. Can we use the power of awareness to heal others? Buddhist healing techniques like Reiki are based on the simple notion that providing attention to parts of the body that need it brings healing.

My teacher had a wonderful explanation. When a child is hurt or is upset, how do we console him? By holding him. It is human instinct to hold a child who is distressed. Both our attention and that of the child's are drawn naturally to the injury. In most cases, we come to the conclusion that the wound will heal just fine. If not, we apply more attention and medicine.

This also applies to mental distress. When our partner is angry or upset, we apply our attention to console them. We listen and commiserate. Bringing our awareness to others is how we can help them heal.

Medical studies show Reiki, a gentle laying on of hands, improves outcomes and speeds healing. It is becoming standard practice in hospitals nationwide. Likewise, prayer is bringing intention, attention, and awareness to those in need of healing. Are there limits to its healing power of awareness?

In Contact

One of the universally recognized symbols of Buddhism is the lotus flower. The metaphor of blossoming represents the ideal of opening up. Opening to experience requires that we break through the boundaries of small mind and its ill effects.

Medicine has its limits. Death is inevitable for each of us. But if we can open ourselves and allow the all-pervading light of Amitabha to shine through, we can be completely present to enjoy the life we have.

When I see a community spontaneously form and bring its attention to someone in need, I see the healing power of Amitabha. When someone in the community is injured, there is a natural desire to reach out and to seek wholeness as a community. Our hearts open, and we reach out for the connection found in community.

The light of Amitabha is very powerful. Boundaries have no meaning, whether it be our head, our bodies, or our community. Being open like flowers is our natural state. Seek its power and enjoy its bliss.

27 Wisdom & Compassion

First, Become a Buddha

The Dalai Lama's twitter account broadcasted a nice, little gem of Buddhist insight the other day. The tweet announced: *Great compassion and wisdom are the chief qualities of the Buddha.*

The Dalai Lama's observation was profound and beautiful. But like most sound bites, it probably concealed more truth than it offered. What does it mean to act with wisdom and compassion? Are we capable of it?

The answer is, of course, *yes*, and *maybe*, and sometimes *no*. The effort to live the Buddha's way of wisdom and compassion reminds me of Steve Martin when he offered this advice:

"How can you become a millionaire? First…get a million dollars."

What's ironic is that while Steve's advice is pretty unhelpful in the world of finance, we can effectively borrow the metaphor for Buddhist cultivation.

How can you act as a Buddha, with wisdom and compassion? First…become a Buddha.

What is a Buddha? The Sanskrit word Buddha means "awakened one." Can we become awake? Of course we can. We are awake now. When we're speaking, working, eating, angry, sad, jubilant, and even simply breathing—we are awake. We are Buddhas.

So, if we are all awake, if we are all Buddhas, why do we sometimes fail to act with wisdom and compassion?

Wake Up

What drew me to Buddhism was the directness in which the Buddha named and took on the difficulties of life. The entree to the practice is directly through personal experience. The Noble Truths point straight to the causes of each and every person's dissatisfaction.

The Buddha's teaching is that, if we wish to forego dissatisfaction, we need to be awake. Being awake and seeing our circumstances clearly are the first steps to acting wisely.

What did the Buddha mean by seeing clearly? It means being directly in touch with our experience. It means spending time in the only place our senses operate; here and now.

We see clearly when; we stop and notice the smell, texture, and taste of our food; we take a few moments to appreciate what those around us are doing to make our lives so rich; we pay attention to the feel of our bodies as we sit at work doing our jobs.

But...how often are we really awake and in the present moment?

The Buddha recommended the practice of meditation for everyone. It's time spent paying attention to the physical and mental activities of our lives. The practice is uniting our senses with the objects of our senses. Our sense of sight with the light of our surroundings. Our sense of smell with the perfume of the here and now. The sense of touch with the sensations of our skin, and so on. It's simply the act of *being* in the most direct way.

Sitting silently and observing the discomfort of our spine as we slump in our seat, allows us to see the causes of our back pain. It tells us to make adjustments in our posture. Doing this a little every day is the path to healing our bodies.

Sitting quietly allows us to observe the myriad thoughts, ideas, and worries that pass through our minds. By doing this, we begin to see how important, or unimportant, these ideas are in relation to what is going on right now. We discover that we are often drawn to these transient thoughts and end up missing the pleasure of our quiet time. Doing this a little every day is a path to healing our minds.

While most of our lives are spent working, and not on a meditation cushion, the insights we gain give us the keys to unlock the power of natural healing and contentment. Noticing our bad posture allows us to relieve our discomfort, clearly seeing life and our relationships can help us be more healthy and happy.

"(I Can't Get No) Satisfaction"

Mick Jagger and Keith Richards

While seeing clearly can be a path to healing and happiness, the opposite is true of being in a dream state.... The Buddha warned us that if we live disconnected from our world, we will be unhappy.

A great example of our disconnect with the world is ideology. When we adhere more and more tightly to an ideology, say politics, we create a divide between ourselves and reality

Look at the consequences. When we argue with someone with a different ideology than our own, we usually end up talking apples to oranges. Each person enumerates the virtues of their beliefs and the vices of others. There is often little room for agreement.

"I never learned from a man who agreed with me."

Robert A. Heinlein

In our minds, ideologies that differ from our own are, by definition, wrong. The more we're convinced of our own truth, coming to an understanding with someone with a differing set of beliefs doesn't seem possible. Tragically, we can arrive at a point where we no longer see our friend as a person, but as the enemy.

At best we depart, agreeing to disagree. At worst we become bitter and angry, and we carry this into our relationships with others. This is suffering.

Et Tu?

Our relationships with our partners can also suffer from being attached to ideas. As our relationships age, we develop habits of being with each other. We develop expectations about how our partners think and feel, based on past experience.

We forfeit communicating and listening in exchange for these notions. We develop a relationship with our expectations. At the same time, we become distant from our partners. With this distance come loneliness, resentment, and unhappiness. When our loved ones do not act or behave as we expect, we become confused, angry, and dissatisfied. Sometimes listening comes too late, and we lose the ones we love.

If being in tune with our senses is wakefulness, then becoming immersed in ideas is dreaming, and as we've seen, this is the cause of suffering.

"Drawn by the Buddha, we return effortlessly to naturalness;

Naturalness is itself the land of Amitabha."

Shinran (Kyogyoshinsho)

In Pure Land Buddhism, we are encouraged to chant the name of the Buddha. Throughout the entire day, we are encouraged to return our minds to the Buddha. The Buddha is our awakened selves. To be a Buddha is to be awake.

If we are mindful of the Buddha (reality), we are drawn to our natural form of being. We are connected with the world.

Wisdom & Compassion

Shinran, the founder of Jodo Shinshu, reminds us that if we are present, the Pure Land of Amitabha Buddha is right here and now. If we are distracted or disconnected from experiences, we will live in our own private hell.

When we see our own propensity for suffering, we will recognize it in others. This is wisdom. Recognizing the causes of suffering in others causes great compassion to arise naturally.

Coming to this realization is both natural and profound. It is the result of the simple act of being awake. Is there any other way for us to be besides being our true selves?

Great compassion and wisdom are our natural qualities, because, of course, we are all Buddha.

28 We're Not Gonna Take It

Listening to Dee Snider scream, "We're not Gonna Take it," can incite anyone to raise a fist. Arnold Schwarzenegger used it as part of an effective campaign in 2003. It's a message that resonates for anyone who is frustrated with the status quo.

For Buddhists, when we take refuge, we are saying the same thing; "We're not going to take it anymore." What "it" is, is suffering.

Fight the Powers That Be

One of my goals as the leader of a Buddhist Sangha is to instill a sense of *Bodhicitta* in the minds and hearts of the people who practice with us. Bodhi is the Sanskrit word for wakefulness. Citta means heart or mind. Bodhicitta means *the awakened mind of compassion.*

Bodhicitta naturally arises as we become attuned with the Buddha's message of suffering and the cause of suffering. If you have ever attended a Buddhist Sangha you've heard the message

It goes like this: Suffering or dissatisfaction is caused by trying to find happiness, but doing it unskillfully.

Our patterns of dissatisfaction are simple. We project happiness onto objects, events, or relationships. We briefly enjoy them, or worse, take them for granted. When they fade or end, we suffer disappointment, regrets, or we feel nothing at all.

We're Fed Up

When we do our practice, and many times fail to affect change in our own lives, we become frustrated. This is why it's crucial to cultivate compassion for ourselves. We recognize our failing, but we also have faith in the Buddha's path. Seeing that we have much hard work to do to succeed even just a little, compassion for ourselves is the logical path. It is the most effective way to remove the obstacle of frustration.

When we reflect on how we all repeatedly suffer, we develop a greater compassion for people who are "fed up" with the way things are, but can't do anything about it.

Buddhism offers many techniques for cultivating lasting contentment. But none of them is any use to anyone without Bodhicitta. Gyaltrul Rinpoche made this wonderfully sharp observation:

> "Without the awakened mind of love and compassion, practicing [advanced techniques] and other kinds of meditation will only make you tired."
>
> Gyaltrul Rinpoche

Awakening the mind of love and compassion can feel like fighting the ocean tide. Our unskillful habits are deeply ingrained. Being fed up seems inevitable. But there are two options; compassion for ourselves and others, or continued suffering.

The World is Crumbling All around Us

What's interesting is that both choices lead in the same direction. If we choose suffering, our efforts to keep pace in the rat race lead us to feel that our lives are crumbling around us. No matter how much time, energy, and resources we invest in this cycle of consumption, we make no progress. We reach a point where we have to say enough is enough.

On the other hand, if we choose the path of wisdom and compassion, our world also comes crumbling down. We begin to recognize that the cause of our suffering is the egocentric world view of materialism and separateness that we have constructed.

Aspiring to Bodhicitta is the first step on the path to enlightenment. Refuge is the first step towards Bodhicitta.

Refuge from the Storm

Refuge is a good choice of words. Because refuge is just that—seeking sanctuary from the endless cycle of dissatisfaction. When we take refuge in the Buddha, the Dharma, and the Sangha, we are not only, saying enough is enough; we're preparing to do something about it

When someone takes refuge, it's seen as an acknowledgement that Buddhism is the path for them. But this is a superficial aspect of refuge. On a deeper level, it is the point where we accept the diagnosis, and we're ready to seek treatment.

When you take refuge based on compassion for yourself and others, it is most auspicious.

As you move from an interest in Buddhism to acquiring the mind of Bodhicitta, consider taking refuge. Say, enough is enough. Tell 'em, you're not gonna take it anymore.

Final Meditation

Making the Choice and Finding the space: This first step is an important one. You are making a choice to seek refuge, even for a moment. This is what commitment looks like. It is one moment at a time. Each moment is a new opportunity to choose peace. Every time you make the choice—that's success.

Go to a space that you find refreshing or invigorating. If it's nice enough, go outside. Ideally find someplace where nature features prominently. Perhaps you can be under a tree, near a flowing body of water, or even a patch of grass. Find a comfortable place to sit or stroll for a few moments.

Settling into your body: If you are standing, stop for a moment and feel the contact between your feet and the earth. If you are sitting, settle firmly onto your hips. Notice the contact with your seat. Inhale deeply and stretch your arms high into the air. Lengthen every part of your body. Open from your ankle to your hips. Find space in your spine all the way to the crown of your head.

On the exhale, let your arms down and notice the brief pause between the breaths. Wait for your body to start the inhale, don't force it.

Settling into the breath: On the next breath, notice the sensation of the air flowing past your nostrils. Feel the breath rise through your nasal cavities, down the back of your throat, and into your lungs. With the rising of your sternum, let your heart float up a little, and notice the joy that can bring. Allow that feeling to emanate from your heart through your entire body. Let it radiate through every pore of your skin. Feel how good it is to be alive.

For this meditation, keep your eyes open to develop an appreciation for your relationship with the world. As every pore of your body tingles with a sense of openness and willingness to engage sensation, notice what your senses are taking in. What sounds do you hear? What smells, textures, temperature and even tastes are you witness to?

Settle into being: As thoughts and other distractions arise, notice them, allow them to run their course. Notice where they came from and where they go. As the distraction dissipates, let your next breath return you to a sense of openness. Discover the pleasure of just being.

For the next 30 breaths, just be. Let each breath open you more and more, there is no limit to your ability to let go.

When you've completed the 30 breaths, continue.

As you've finished this final meditation, take a moment to appreciate the peace that is always available to you. Notice the gratitude that can naturally arise. Acknowledge the contrast between daily life and these moments of clarity. Develop a sense of compassion for yourself and others in recognition that we all suffer every day for lack of clarity. From that wellspring of compassion, commit to the path of the Buddha. Commit to live the examined life of the eightfold path. Commit to find the source of lasting love, joy, equanimity, and peace.

> May all beings have happiness and its causes,
>
> May all be free from unhappiness and its causes,
>
> May all dwell in equanimity, free from attraction and aversion,
>
> May all quickly find the great happiness which lies beyond all misery,
>
> May all enjoy inner and outer peace, now and forever.
>
> Namo Amitofo

About The Author

Andrew Furst is an author, meditation teacher, yogi, backup guitarist for his teenage boys, a lucky husband, and a software project guy.

www.andrewfurst.net

31003788R00069

Made in the USA
Charleston, SC
03 July 2014